UNVEILED

INSIDE IRAN'S #WOMANLIFEFREEDOM REVOLT

JONATHAN HAROUNOFF

Black Rose Writing | Texas

©2025 by Jonathan Harounoff
All rights reserved. No part of this book may be reproduced, stored in a retrieval system or transmitted in any form or by any means without the prior written permission of the publishers, except by a reviewer who may quote brief passages in a review to be printed in a newspaper, magazine or journal.

The author grants the final approval for this literary material.

First printing

Some names and identifying details may have been changed to protect the privacy of individuals

ISBN: 978-1-68513-652-9 (Paperback); 978-1-68513-688-8 (Hardcover)
LIBRARY OF CONGRESS CONTROL NUMBER: 2025934456
PUBLISHED BY BLACK ROSE WRITING
www.blackrosewriting.com

Printed in the United States of America
Suggested Retail Price (SRP) $18.95 (Paperback); $25.95 (Hardcover)

Unveiled is printed in Garamond Premier Pro

*As a planet-friendly publisher, Black Rose Writing does its best to eliminate unnecessary waste to reduce paper usage and energy costs, while never compromising the reading experience. As a result, the final word count vs. page count may not meet common expectations.

Cover art: Stephanie Posner

For my inspiring wife, Stephanie, who has been there every step of the way.

And to the brave Iranian women and men who fought—and fight—for freedom and dignity.

PRAISE FOR
UNVEILED

"*Unveiled* takes us inside the 'Woman, Life, Freedom' movement, sparked by the slaying of a young woman for wearing a loose hijab, in what became the most serious challenge the regime has faced in forty-six years. Harounoff has given us a nonfiction drama replete with heroines and villains, one that is sure to captivate readers."
—PETER KANN, Pulitzer Prize-winning foreign correspondent and former publisher, *The Wall Street Journal*

"This groundbreaking book provides readers with a unique and frightening glimpse into Iran's totalitarian regime. Expertly researched and engagingly presented, *Unveiled* is an essential source for scholars, policymakers, and all those interested in understanding contemporary Iran."
—MICHAEL OREN, former Israeli ambassador to the United States

"The regime may have brutally crushed the women-led democracy movement in Iran, but the movement is far from dead. It will be back and ultimately prevail. That is the hopeful message of *Unveiled*. The country is at a turning point and Harounoff shows us what a new Iran might look like."
—ARI L. GOLDMAN, Professor Emeritus, Columbia University Graduate School of Journalism

"Through heart-wrenching testimonies, *Unveiled* tells us about the women and girls who fought back. *Unveiled* is indispensable reading about the real-life freedom fighters who risked their lives after the murder of Mahsa Jina Amini. This book goes beyond the failure of the movement and, for the first time, explores why it fell short in toppling the regime."
—NEGAR MOJTAHEDI, Iran International journalist

"*Unveiled* delves into the Mahsa Amini uprising's global impact and its potential to shape a new Iran. Harounoff vividly portrays the unwavering resilience and courage of the Iranian people in the face of the regime's repression. It is no longer a question of 'if' a new Iran will emerge but 'when.'"
—NAZENIN ANSARI, publisher and managing editor, Kayhan London

"*Unveiled* is a definitive account of the most powerful protest movement the Islamic regime in Iran has ever faced. While the regime's support and funding of terrorist organizations abroad is well known, the terrorism this regime has waged against its own citizens—particularly against women—has garnered far less attention.

In *Unveiled*, Harounoff writes with depth and compassion of the forces leading the courageous movement for women's rights in Iran. I recommend *Unveiled* to anyone who wishes to better understand the people of Iran and their struggle for freedom."

–YARDENA SCHWARTZ, author of *Ghosts of a Holy War: The 1929 Massacre in Palestine That Ignited the Arab-Israeli Conflict*

"In *Unveiled*, Jonathan Harounoff provides an absorbing account of the origins and legacy of the 'Woman, Life, Freedom' protest movement. This book is an accessible and immensely moving addition to the existing literature on modern Iran and its fascinating history of protest culture.

Unveiled is unique in that it does not only set out in meticulous detail the historic events that took place in Iran after the death of Mahsa Jina Amini, but also examines why the movement, for all its successes, ultimately fell short in its ultimate goal of bringing down the regime. While this protest movement may have failed, Iranians continue to take to the streets. It's only a matter of time before this regime ends up on the ash heap of history."

–MARK DUBOWITZ, CEO, Foundation for Defense of Democracies

"*Unveiled* offers a look at the promise of the 'Woman, Life, Freedom' movement. This movement is far from over. It has just started. While the Islamic Republic remains in power, countless Iranians are engaging in brave acts of civil disobedience on a daily basis. *Unveiled* pulls back the curtain on the powerful transformations taking place in Iranian society."

–JASON BRODSKY, policy director, United Against Nuclear Iran

"*Unveiled* is an important work of investigative journalism that dissects one of the most consequential protest movements of the modern Middle East. Harounoff's storytelling places readers on the streets of Iran as bullets from the Revolutionary Guard target women—and in the halls of Washington where decision-makers and the Iranian diaspora tried, and then failed, to forge a consensus opposition movement.

Unveiled provides a critical introspection on how the Islamic Republic of Iran lost its base of public support and how Ayatollah Ali Khamenei learned from the lessons of the Soviet Union, Tiananmen Square, and the Islamic Revolution itself to stave off the nascent revolution. As the dark forces of radical and misogynistic totalitarianism envelop more of the Middle East, *Unveiled* is an important tribute to the movements fighting back, and a thoughtful reflection of the ways they have yet to go."
–**GABRIEL NORONHA, former special advisor on Iran, U.S. State Department**

"An emotional must-read for anyone looking to understand the rise and impact of Iran's latest protest movement seeking all-out revolution. Harounoff's work is thoroughly researched and is a highly readable account of the brave and fearless women, men and youth who seek to bring an end to the Islamic Republic."
–**ELLIE COHANIM, former deputy Special Envoy to Monitor and Combat Antisemitism, U.S. State Department**

"The story of Mahsa Amini is rooted in the courage of youth tested and challenged by unimaginable circumstances that demand the utmost moral clarity in a world that has seemingly forgotten what that means. Youthful curiosity—and bravery—are what make Jonathan Harounoff's writing so important. Three years after Mahsa Amini's death, her legacy will not be forgotten, and Harounoff is front and center in this crucial effort. *Unveiled* reveals the personal motivations and historical factors that went into Amini's own defiance at the hands of Iranian mullahs—as well as how and why the movement she inspired captured the imagination of so many and so strongly."
–**DAVID CHRISTOPHER KAUFMAN, columnist and editor,** *New York Post*

"*Unveiled: Inside Iran's #WomanLifeFreedom Revolt* is a powerful chronicle of courage and hope, documenting an extraordinary grassroots movement led by women in Iran. Jonathan Harounoff masterfully weaves personal narratives with historical context, illuminating the tireless fight against the oppressive regime of the Islamic Republic. His seasoned writing captures the essence of a global revolution, where women, supported by men, inspire collective resistance and change. This compelling book is a testament to the indomitable human spirit and a must-read for anyone passionate about freedom and equality."
–LISA DAFTARI, editor-in-chief, The Foreign Desk

"*Unveiled* is both heartbreaking and inspiring. I recommend this book to anyone looking to understand in encyclopedic detail the decades-long threat the Islamic Republic has posed not just to global stability, but to its own people."
–BENI SABTI, Iran researcher, The Institute for National Security Studies

"The fight for liberty in Iran is complex, personal, and urgent, and the story of its people's ongoing struggle for freedom is one the world cannot afford to ignore. Unveiled draws attention to the people behind the headlines with care and purpose, as Iran faces a defining moment in its modern history."
– JONATHAN SACERDOTI, award-winning writer and broadcaster

"Jonathan Harounoff has a knack for telling human stories while also grasping the broader sociopolitical context. As he follows Iranians who wish to remake their country and take it back from the ruling elite, he gives us a glimpse not just to their bravery and heroism, but to the future they are building, often away from the headlines."
–ARASH AZIZI, historian and author of *What Iranians Want: Women, Life, Freedom*

CONTENTS

EARLY CHRONOLOGY OF THE MAHSA AMINI PROTESTS	
PREFACE	
THE PERILS OF PUNCTUATION	1
MAHSA'S MOMENT	10
ZAN, ZENDEGI, AZADI	17
A CULTURE OF PROTEST: FROM CROWN TO TURBAN	34
SOCIAL MEDIA IN IRAN	50
CREATIVE RESISTANCE IN MUSIC, ART AND DANCE	66
THE DUEL IN DOHA	79
A DICTATOR'S DILEMMA	94
THE OPPOSITION	115
EPILOGUE: WAITING FOR THE REVOLUTION	132
ENDNOTES	141
ABOUT THE AUTHOR	
ACKNOWLEDGEMENTS	

NOTE ON TERMINOLOGY AND TRANSLITERATION

Unveiled contains conventional English spellings for Persian words and names commonly found in the English-language press. I, the author, am responsible for all translations in this book, except for those otherwise credited in the notes. For the transliteration of Persian words in this book, I opted for the simplest forms that match the vernacular.

UNVEILED

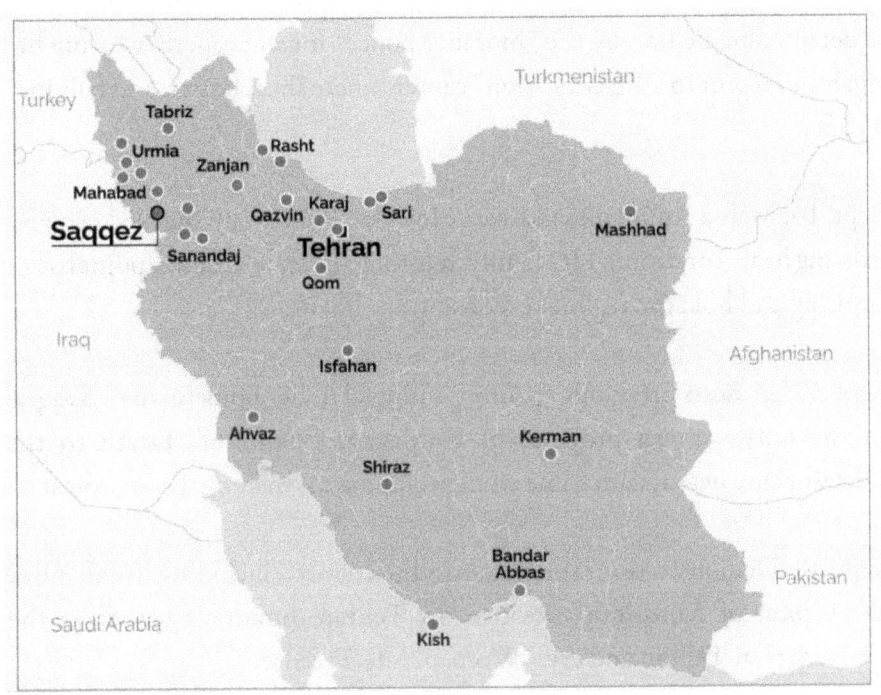

Key centers of protest following Mahsa Amini's death in September 2022. Map source: Italian Institute for International Political Studies (ISPI), Agence France-Presse (AFP), Amwaj, 2022.

EARLY CHRONOLOGY OF
THE MAHSA AMINI PROTESTS

2022

Sept. 13: Twenty-two-year-old Mahsa Amini, from Iran's Kurdistan region, is detained in Tehran by the "morality police" for improperly wearing her hijab and is sent to a "re-education" center, where she is beaten and falls into a coma.

Sept. 16: Mahsa Amini dies in Kasra Hospital. Police state she died of a pre-existing heart condition. Her family, rejecting the state's claims, point to her bruising and hold the regime responsible for her death.

Sept. 17: Protests break out at Amini's funeral in her hometown of Saqqez, in the northwestern province of Kurdistan. Chants of "Death to the Dictator" are heard, with some women ripping off their hijabs in protest.

Sept. 18: Demonstrations spread across the country, including to Sanandaj, the capital of Kurdistan province. In Tehran, hundreds gather at the University of Tehran and cry, "Woman, Life, Freedom."

Sept. 19: Students at three college campuses in Tehran—Amirkabir University, Shahid Beheshti University and Tehran University—stage rallies.

Sept. 19: The hashtag, "#mahsaamini," is mentioned two million times on Twitter, becoming one of the most popular Persian-language hashtags in social media history.

Sept. 20: Outbursts of protest intensify further, including in Bandar Abbas, Hamedan, Kermanshah, Qom and Tabriz.

Sept. 21: Government authorities begin to curb Internet services, as well as access to social media platforms like Instagram and WhatsApp.

Sept. 25: Daily protests are documented in thirty of Iran's thirty-one provinces.

Sept 29: The body of sixteen-year-old Nika Shakarami is discovered in a morgue by her family nine days after she went missing during a protest in Tehran. Autopsies suggest she had been bludgeoned to death. Government officials claim she fell from a four-story building.

Sept 29: Iranian singer Shervin Hajipour, whose song *Baraye* became the unofficial anthem of the "Woman, Life, Freedom" protest movement, is arrested in Tehran.

Sept. 30: Security forces kill sixty-six people in Zahedan, southeastern Iran, in a crackdown known as "Bloody Friday."

Oct. 3: Supreme Leader Ali Khamenei speaks out for the first time since the protests broke out, describing Amini's death as a "bitter incident" malevolently orchestrated by Iran's enemies abroad.

Oct. 8: Female students at Al-Zahra University shout "Raisi, get lost" at former President Ebrahim Raisi during an official visit to the university campus.

Oct. 9: In an attempt to disrupt the unrest, government officials shut down schools in Kurdistan province.

Oct. 10: Oil refinery workers across Iran, including in Abadan and Kangan, go on strike.

Oct. 14: Protesters in Zahedan stage a massive demonstration marking two weeks since the "Bloody Friday" massacre.

Oct. 22: Approximately 100,000 people march in Berlin in solidarity with the protesters in Iran. Thousands more march in cities worldwide, including London, Paris, Toronto, Los Angeles, Tokyo and Sydney.

Nov. 11: Players on Iran's national basketball team refrain from singing the national anthem during a match against China, in a show of solidarity with Iranian protesters back home.

Nov. 17: Protesters set fire to the ancestral home of Ayatollah Ruhollah Khomeini, the founder and first Supreme Leader of the Islamic Republic, in the city of Khomeyn.

Dec. 8: Twenty-two-year-old barista and protester Mohsen Shekari is executed by the Islamic Republic on spurious charges of blocking a street in Tehran and injuring a security officer. Shekari's death marked the first known execution of a protester from the Mahsa Amini protests.

Dec. 14: The United Nations' Economic and Social Council (ECOSOC) votes overwhelmingly in favor of expelling the Islamic Republic of Iran from the U.N. Commission on the Status of Women.

PREFACE

Iran—the country, history, culture, and politics—has always been a part of my life. My grandparents on both sides hail from the Jewish community of Mashhad, known as "the holiest city in Iran," located in the far northeast near Turkmenistan. I've never visited Iran. It's been unadvisable for Jewish Brits since 1979, but I grew up listening to Persian, surrounded by Persian carpets, music and food. My favorites include staples like *tahdig*, crispy rice infused with saffron; *ghormeh sabzi*, a Persian stew consisting of meat, green herbs, beans and dried limes; as well as meatballs made out of lamb or chicken known as *gondi*.

Jewish history in Iran had traumatic, painful elements to it. Yet there's also a huge sense of pride and attachment to Iran that Jewish Iranians still feel, oftentimes exhibiting a complete dissociation between the country of Iran, with thousands of years of rich history and civilization, and the forty-six-year-old Islamic Republic of Iran. Like many in the diaspora, my family saw the authoritarian regime as not so much leading, but occupying, Iran for nearly five decades. In the aftermath of the Islamic Revolution of 1979, tens of thousands of Persian Jews left Iran, with the population dwindling from 80,000 then to around 10,000 today, making it still, remarkably, the second-largest Jewish population in the Middle East after Israel.

At college, I took Persian classes, delved into Middle Eastern history, and began writing about Iran for international publications. This book became a natural progression—writing about a place that has fascinated me since childhood.

That said, writing this book was no small endeavor. How do you encapsulate recent events in Iran in 200 pages? How do you write a book about a region that is shifting every day?

Though trained as a journalist, my focus is, fortunately, somewhat different from that of a reporter chasing the next story. Middle East news bulletins seldom exclude the Islamic Republic of Iran. More often than not, though, the theocracy is characterized in mainstream media as an anti-Western regime pursuing an aggressive foreign policy agenda hellbent on achieving nuclear weapons and annihilating the State of Israel. Or as a state-sponsor of regional terror through its proxy militias, Hamas, Hezbollah and the Houthis.

Far less attention is placed on my book's focus: the quotidian happenings inside Iran affecting ordinary Iranians. The lack of interest in the everyday perhaps explains why Western media seldom draws enough of a distinction between the Islamic Republic and the people of Iran. *Unveiled* sheds light on—and honors—the irrepressibly brave Iranians, young and old, male and female, religious and non-observant, who never stopped fighting for a brighter future. For dignity. For women. For life. For freedom.

Jonathan Harounoff
New York
December 2024

CHAPTER 1
THE PERILS OF PUNCTUATION

In May 2024, the Iranian writer and activist Hossein Shanbehzadeh replied to a tweet on the social media platform X with a simple grammatical correction: a single period at the end of a sentence. In most countries, his edit might be seen as snarky at worst. In Iran, he was arrested and thrown into prison.

Shanbehzadeh's crime was correcting a post on the account of Iran's Supreme Leader Ali Khamenei that featured a photo of the octogenarian premier posing with the national student volleyball team. The accompanying caption was, in fact, missing a period at the end of the sentence. However, in Iran, the Supreme Leader occupies a near god-like role. He is not someone to copyedit publicly. Worse, Shanbehzadeh's reply quickly went viral, receiving far more engagement than Khamenei's own tweet. Thousands of people commented on Shanbehzadeh's post with a supportive punctuation mark of their own.

Shanbehzadeh also had a history of political activism. In fact, it had only been a few months since his last term in prison ended, a sentence during which he was allegedly beaten and flogged.[1] His previous charge stemmed from his involvement in the 2019 anti-government wave of protests. His past activism probably weighed against him when Iranian authorities condemned him to a prison sentence of twelve years for his act of grammatical insubordination.[2] Shanbehzadeh remained defiant, nonetheless. "I am an innocent prisoner. My phone privileges have been revoked. I cannot call my mother without an intermediary," he said, speaking from Tehran's notorious Evin Prison.³ Political dissidents have been held in often harsh conditions at Evin since the 1970s during the reign of the Shah.

The consequences of a single dot on a social media platform highlight several tendencies of modern Iranian society. The first is how, in a repressive state, the smallest everyday actions are celebrated as acts of resistance. The second is the critical role of social media in recent protests and popular resistance to a regime ultimately helmed by the Supreme Leader. The third is the severe overreaction of a government to these tiny, but explosive, acts of rebellion—efforts that belie a degree of paranoia on the part of a government that is increasingly out-of-touch, even reviled, by large segments of the Iranian population.

While the government may have been paranoid, it was also correct that Iranians perceived some sort of anti-regime message in Shanbehzadeh's pedantry. Some saw his minimalist reply as a correction, a critique, of the country's leader. Others saw in the dot a deeper meaning, representing the end of something, perhaps that of the Islamic Republic—a threat the regime had been violently thwarting for years, with the most recent major revolts flaring up in mid-September 2022.

Those protests in late 2022 had also sprung from unremarkable beginnings: an ordinary young woman, Mahsa Amini, in her early twenties—not an outspoken activist or a celebrity—was visiting family in Tehran when she had the misfortune of crossing the *Gasht-e Ershad*, Iran's morality police. Amini's arrest included the all-too-ordinary experience, particularly for women, of being harassed about what she was wearing, followed by a massive, violent overreaction by state forces and a subsequent storm of criticism amplified and globalized by social media. But it was precisely the woman's ordinariness that made her subsequent death at the hands of the morality police so impactful to Iranians around the country and beyond.

Mahsa Jina Amini hadn't traveled to Tehran to become a martyr. She hadn't expected her name to become the most trending Twitter hashtag of all time. She didn't aspire to have her face light up Times Square in New York or have streets in Los Angeles and Vienna named after her. She never anticipated that she would be the spark that set off the most serious challenge to the country's hardline clerics since they took power in 1979. Yet, within days of her death, Amini was known by everyone inside Iran, especially women who knew that it could have been them. Overnight, she became a global icon.

The "Woman, Life, Freedom" movement, ignited by Amini's killing, did not succeed in toppling the Islamic Republic of Iran. But the country will never be the same again. The revolutionary spirit that Iranians have since shown remains inextinguishable. Three years on, women continue to defy mandatory headscarf rules by walking on Iran's streets with their hair partially or totally uncovered. But their unveiling goes far beyond a defiant hairstyle. It is an unambiguous repudiation of one of the central pillars of the Islamic Republic that have stood firm for more than forty-six years.

Throughout the Islamic Republic's history, itself born out of the 1979 Revolution that toppled the Shah, waves of dissent and protest have become commonplace. In recent decades, crippling inflation, stagnant wages, high unemployment rates, systemic corruption, police brutality, water shortages and exorbitant fuel and food prices have all brought Iranians into the streets. But none have posed an existential threat to the country's theocratic system of government in the same way as the latest wave of protests in September 2022 caused by the death of a twenty-two-year-old Kurdish woman.

The end of Amini's life was the beginning of something extraordinary. It was a death that acquired its own stratospheric significance, with ramifications that continue to reverberate well into 2025. It began a movement that unleashed pent-up social unrest brewing for decades in a country increasingly isolated and cut off from much of the Western world. It brought to life a cacophony of sympathy and outrage, expressed worldwide in art, music, song and dance: from the corridors of the United Nations, the White House and the UK Parliament, to the Oscars, Grammys, and Paris Fashion Week.

In the months following Mahsa Amini's death, the Islamic Republic struggled to curb the masses of women walking the streets and riding the metro without headscarves. The regime retreated. Removing the hijab had become a symbol not just of resistance, but of regime change, and women stood at the vanguard of this antigovernment wave of protests.

Despite violent government crackdowns on protesters, including retaliatory executions, as well as temporary internet outages, Iranian netizens harnessed the globality of social media to document this historic moment. What made the protests in Iran even more remarkable was that they were spearheaded not by men but by women, girls and minority groups, including Kurds, Arabs, Turks, Baluchis, Lurs and others, who united across religious and ethnic lines to call for an end to the clerical gerontocracy in Tehran. "From Zahedan to Kurdistan, may my life be sacrificed for Iran," so went a popular slogan that went viral nationwide.

For the first time in the Middle East, women and young girls served as the engine driving a popular uprising against the iron rule of the Islamic Republic. The youth, who had largely stayed out of previous waves of unrest in recent decades, now stood at the forefront of the Mahsa Amini protests, aware that their future prospects were bleak under the Islamic Republic. Their predominantly secular aspirations, informed by social media, sharply contrasted with that of the theocratic state.

In early October 2022, Ali Fadavi, deputy commander of the powerful Islamic Revolutionary Guard Corps (IRGC) claimed the average age of an arrested protester was fifteen.[4] That's not to say the country's older generation stood in opposition to the movement's goals. Far from it. Though many of the country's older generation subscribed to the "Woman, Life, Freedom" movement, traumatic memories from the promise—and ultimate disappointment—of the 1979 revolution still haunted them. Unlike younger generations unshackled by the past, the regime's callous and uncompromising response to dissent meant revolts carried a certain futility among more senior Iranians.

Despite severe internet outages in some parts of the country, Iran's youth are more connected to their global peers than any generation before. Through the democratizing power of the internet and social media, they have been exposed to different ways of life worldwide, mostly through virtual private networks (VPNs) that bypass government-enforced restrictions online, and have learned of progressive social reforms taking place in other conservative Islamic societies such as Saudi Arabia, which in recent years relaxed its laws on dress codes, mandatory gender segregation, and unaccompanied female drivers.

The protests in Iran rattled two central pillars of the Islamic Republic that were once seen as unshakeable: the country's irrevocable animosity toward archenemies Israel and the United States, and its stringent hijab laws, which prescribe conservative dress codes—covering nearly their entire body, including their hair—for females as young as seven. (Some lesser prohibitions extend to men's dress, like wearing sleeveless shirts and shorts). Keeping women veiled was so defining a symbol for the Islamic Republic that Ruhollah Khomeini, the father of the Islamic Revolution of 1979, described it as the "flag of the revolution." For the Islamic Republic, the mandatory hijab was not just about dressing modestly. The veil represented submission and control. "The compulsory hijab law isn't just about controlling women's bodies—it's about controlling our ability to think for ourselves," said Nasrin Sotoudeh, an Iranian human rights attorney described by some as the "Nelson Mandela of Iran."[5]

While the same regime still stands, the women-led revolutionary movement that began in 2022 has led to some promising change in the country, with one Western diplomat in Tehran estimating that, by September 2023, around one in five women were now openly flouting the Islamic Republic's conservative dress laws by going out onto the streets unveiled.[6]

More importantly, unlike past waves of civil unrest in Iran in recent years and decades, these protesters called for more than the end of the hijab laws or reforms to the Islamic theocracy. What began as a movement over the freedom of women's bodies turned into a broader movement demanding greater social and political freedoms. Instead of chanting for electoral reforms within the framework of the regime, Iranians called for the demise of the Supreme Leader, Ayatollah Ali Khamenei, who has ruled Iran since 1989, and for a new system of government to supplant the Islamic Republic.

It took many months before regime authorities were able to violently subdue protesters. Yet despite the violence inflicted on protesters, the regime was unable to suppress the revolutionary mood that has since swept the country.

In the massive 2009 protests over the disputed reelection of Mahmoud Ahmadinejad, reform of the system of the Islamic Republic was the ultimate goal for protesters. After Mahsa's death, transformative and total regime change became the focus. "After Mahsa, everything is hanging by a hair." This slogan, spray-painted on a wall in Tehran in late September 2022, encapsulated the unprecedented fury and appetite for change felt by Iranians.[7]

As the protests roared, the Supreme Leader encountered what experts like Karim Sadjadpour describe as a "dictator's dilemma," whereby if his regime continues to remain hostile to change, the protests will continue to grow, but any semblance of acquiescence would enfeeble Ayatollah Khamenei, thereby galvanizing protesters even further.[8] Such a conundrum may involve considerable political calculations and more of a balancing act in other countries.

When intense protests broke out in Libya in 2011 against Muammar Gaddafi's forty-two-years of rule, the dictator doubled down on repression and ended up being overthrown and killed by opposition forces in the northern city of Sirte. Conversely, in 1991, just six years after Mikhail Gorbachev came into power as General Secretary of the Community Party and introduced groundbreaking reforms to transform the Soviet Union, the empire collapsed.

In Iran, the regime has invariably opted for uninterrupted rule through unrelenting, violent repression. That's why these protests, much like past episodes of civil unrest during Ayatollah Khamenei's reign, have been met with brutal violence, imprisonment and, in some cases, executions. Murmurs of compromise or remorse, occasionally reported by journalists and Iran watchers, were quickly negated.

More than five hundred protesters have been killed by regime forces since the protests first erupted in September 2022, including scores of women and children. And tens of thousands of protesters and dissidents sit in jail cells, either indefinitely or until they are summoned for a kangaroo trial that seals their fate. Those jailed include journalists, celebrity actors, chefs and rappers, many of whom were convicted of the catch-all crimes of "corruption on earth" and "waging war against God."

Iran boasts the second-highest rate of executions in the world. On top of executing dissidents linked to the Mahsa Amini protests, 2023 saw Iran's government embark on a vicious execution spree, with at least 853 people executed across the country, a 48 percent increase from 2022 and the highest number since 2015.[9] At least 481 of those executions were related to drug-related offenses, in large part attributed to former President Ebrahim Raisi's declared war on drugs and following Gholamhossein Mohseni-Ejei's appointment as the Head of the Judiciary in 2021.[10] Both had a long track record of punishing dissenters with the death penalty in the years leading up to the 2022-2023 uprising. Raisi had developed a reputation as a merciless member of the Islamic Republic's judiciary with a penchant for capital punishment, known by his ominous moniker as the "hanging judge." He was also a prominent member of the "death committee" purge in Tehran in 1998, comprising religious judges, prosecutors, and intelligence officials, who sentenced thousands of dissident political prisoners to death in arbitrary trials typically lasting no longer than a few minutes.[11] These mass executions earned Raisi another nickname: "The Butcher of Tehran."

The Mahsa Amini protests also erupted at a time of creeping, unavoidable transition. Reports swirled last summer that, at eighty-six, the aging premier Ayatollah Ali Khamenei was facing his second bout of cancer, following treatment for prostate cancer in 2014. With no clear successor in sight, except for his son, Mojtaba, who plays a key role in the Supreme Leader's secretariat, the backdrop for a successful revolution appears as ripe as ever. Several religious figures and military leaders have already spoken out against dynastic succession, especially given that, ironically, the Islamic Republic was a result of a revolution against absolute power held by the monarchy. That revolution in 1979 brought an end to more than 2,000 years of dynastic rule in Iran.

The economic backdrop within which these protests spawned is also worth considering. With the country's economy in the doldrums, combined with the regime's mismanagement and corruption, Iran's economy was stagnating in 2022. Unemployment was high. One-third of Iranians lived below the poverty line.¹² The country's per capita GDP had plummeted, falling from $7,800 in 2011 to $2,300 in 2020. Inflation was skyrocketing, and the lingering effects of the COVID-19 pandemic were still being felt across the country, setting the stage for nationwide unrest. Double-digit inflation was a new phenomenon for some countries in 2022. In Iran, it was the norm. By 2022, the cost of goods and services increased by 1,135 percent over the past decade. The U.S. withdrawal from the nuclear deal (known formally as the Joint Comprehensive Plan of Action) under President Donald Trump in 2018 led to further isolation for the Iranian economy on the international scene, impoverishing even the country's middle class.¹³

The country's currency continued to fall to new lows against the U.S. dollar, driven by crippling protests, strikes at key bazaars and oil facilities, and growing isolation over its nuclear program, human rights abuses and drone supplies to Russia for its war in Ukraine. Two weeks into the Mahsa Amini protests in late September 2022, the Iranian rial had lost 80 percent of its value since 2018, when President Trump withdrew from the 2015 nuclear deal and reimposed American sanctions on Iran.

The Iranian regime, in customary fashion, blamed the currency's precipitous decline in value—and the protest movement overall—on nefarious foreign agents, notably Israel and the U.S., intent on destabilizing the Islamic Republic.

Iran's woeful economy was a serious pain point for Iranians marching in the streets, but the 2022-2023 protests were about much more than that. That's why the economy didn't feature in the movement's most well-known battle cries of "Woman, Life, Freedom" or "Down with the dictator." Rather, the movement represented the first real attempt to completely upend the Islamic Republic and its forty-six-year war on women. It represented a wholesale rejection of forced theocratic government and Islamic strictures in place of choice.

By 2025, the protests in Iran have largely subsided, but the embers of revolutionary spirit are far from extinguished. Once again, the Islamic Republic managed to survive a scare that threatened to paralyze its very existence, first with debilitating Western sanctions and overwhelming domestic unrest.

An unstructured opposition movement—both within Iran and abroad—combined with a brutal retaliation campaign carried out by the Islamic Republic's security forces may explain why the "Woman, Life, Freedom" movement didn't achieve its ultimate revolutionary goal. The Islamic Republic's leaders know that its citizens pose the greatest risk to their existence. That's why any whiff of dissent is met with extreme brutality.

But Iranians, inside Iran and abroad, are still optimistic of a full-blown revolution in the not-too-distant future. To them, Mahsa and the hundreds of young Iranians who lost their lives represent a generation of fearless, ordinary Iranians in search of a better life, resolute in their hopes for a freer Iran. An Iran that's once again part of the global community. An Iran that prioritizes domestic interests and the prosperity of its own people over a damaging foreign policy that has turned it into an international pariah on par with North Korea.

Drawing on exclusive interviews, original reporting, English- and Persian-language social media postings and previously untapped sources, *Unveiled* serves as a detailed account of one of the most consequential and potentially transformative examples of civic protest to have rocked the Middle East in recent history.

The lasting impact of these protests will likely not be known for years to come. One thing is for sure: Iranians will continue to fight for freedom at whatever cost, even if it leads to jailing, torture, sexual assault, or worse.

The Islamic Republic has survived trials and tribulations, both domestic and foreign, since its founding. It has survived more than four decades of intermittent popular unrest and international pressure that, at times, appeared insurmountable. But it has endured.

At the same time, the people of Iran have endured hardship and have revolted with greater frequency and intensity. The "Woman, Life, Freedom" protest movement fell short of achieving its ambitious political goal of regime collapse. But in a country as tempestuous as Iran, all it takes is another spark to ignite a popular, and maybe terminal, uprising.

CHAPTER 2
MAHSA'S MOMENT

"I will not allow my daughter's blood to be trampled on."[14]
–Amjad Amini, father of Mahsa Amini, 2022

At around 6:00 p.m. on the evening of Tuesday, September 13, 2022, a twenty-two-year-old woman stepped onto the escalator at Tehran's Shahid Haghani metro station. She was wearing a long black and white coat, white sneakers, and a black headscarf, often called a hijab, that concealed most of her hair.[15] Mahsa Amini, also known by her Kurdish name Jina or Zhina, was an avid volleyball player and certified swim coach. In recent photos, she wore precisely applied deep red lipstick; a friend of hers described her as "never being able to decide on just one nail polish."[16] As a child, Amini had set up her bedroom as a doctor's office where she tended to her stuffed animals. In a few weeks, she would begin a microbiology program at university, on her way to realizing her professional dream of becoming a doctor. She had traveled to the Iranian capital from her hometown of Saqqez, a small city on the banks of a river that runs through the mountains of Kurdistan, with her seventeen-year-old brother, Kiarash Amini, and their two cousins before her university courses began.

After emerging from the station into the bright early evening sun, Amini and her three family members headed toward nearby Taleghani Forest Park, in the elevated Abbas Abad hills of northern Tehran. The park's hiking trails, picnic areas, and city views are popular among locals and tourists looking for an escape from the city's bustle and heat. The striking views of the snow-capped Alborz mountain range from Tabiat Bridge, a striking modern structure linking Taleghani with another nearby park, make the bridge a favorite spot for snapping Instagram pictures. Because of its higher altitude, Taleghani can also be several degrees cooler than the lower-lying southern portions of the city, offering some relief to Amini who, like most other women in Tehran, was dressed more appropriately for winter in the stifling late summer heat.

Soon after leaving the metro station, Amini, her brother and two cousins, were accosted by the *Gasht-e Ershad*, Iran's morality police. Officers from this force, who had been patrolling the streets to enforce modest clothing since 2005, were recognizable by their white-and-green-striped vans. The team that approached Amini consisted of two women—who wore loose, black robes with long black *chadors* wrapped around their heads, revealing only their faces—and two male officers, wearing dark green military-style uniforms and hats. One of the female officers reportedly called the team's attention to Mahsa Amini's outfit, from which she thought too much hair was protruding. The officers told Amini she would have to go back to the station with them for a brief tutorial on Islamic dress code.

Members of the *Gasht-e Ershad* then grabbed Amini and began forcing her into their van, at which point her brother, Kiarash, tried to intervene. He knew that, whatever the officers claimed, his sister was not safe in the custody of the morality police. One of the male officers twisted his arm behind his back and reassured him that his sister would be free after she attended the hour-long re-education class at Vozara police station. Overpowered, Kiarash watched the van disappear down the city street before setting off to meet his sister after her detainment.

Outside the police station, Kiarash waited anxiously with the relatives of the sixty or so other women who had been picked up by the morality police, many of them holding more conservative clothes for their detained loved ones. After a few women were released onto the street, the crowd heard screams from inside and swarmed the station, banging on its doors. Soon afterwards, officers came out of the station and assaulted members of the anxious crowd.

"All of a sudden, the agents rushed out of the building and attacked us with batons and teargas," Kiarash said. A few minutes later, he saw an ambulance drive away from the building. As more detained women left the building, he heard them saying that someone inside had been killed. Kiarash showed a photo of his sister to one of the women who nodded and said that she had been next to her when it happened.[17]

Shocked, Kiarash asked a nearby soldier what had happened. The soldier claimed that another soldier had been injured and taken to the hospital. Unconvinced, Kiarash ran to nearby Kasra Hospital. A little after 8:00 p.m. on Tuesday, about two hours after Mahsa Amini had been abducted while strolling to the park, doctors told her brother that Mahsa had suffered from an unexpected heart attack and stroke at the police station. Although her heart continued to beat, her brain was no longer functioning.[18]

Mahsa Goes Viral

When Kiarash was able to visit his sister's room, he saw signs of physical abuse. Severe bruising showed on her head, and her left ear was patched to staunch the bleeding. After photos of Mahsa Amini in the hospital appeared online, Iranian doctors noted that, while they didn't have access to Amini's medical file, her injuries appeared to be consistent with the symptoms of severe head trauma.

Despite state attempts at censorship, Amini's story quickly spread across social media inside and, just as importantly, outside of Iran. In Istanbul, Sajjad Khodakarami, an Iranian journalist who had fled state repression two months prior, came across an Instagram story posted by someone who had interviewed people in Kasra Hospital soon after Amini had been admitted. When I spoke to Khodakarami via FaceTime in early 2024, he explained that, soon after the Instagram story appeared, the original poster was told by authorities that he had to remove his content. But Khodakarami, reporting from outside the influence of Iranian authorities, was able to re-circulate the news in his own Instagram post, making him among the first journalists to report on Amini's critical condition after her arrest.

As Amini's story went viral, Iranians started to gather outside the hospital, despite a heavy security presence, including anti-riot trucks. The crowd's anger was palpable. One woman in the crowd, captured on video, shouted, "Where in Islam does it say you have the right to kill?"[19]

Over the following days, Amini's fate continued to capture the attention, and fears, of the country. By Friday, September 16, three days after Amini's detention and the subsequent social media storm, mourners dressed in black began gathering in Argentina Square near Kasra Hospital. Later that day, Niloofar Hamedi, a reporter at the reformist newspaper *Shargh Daily* who had managed to gain access into the hospital, posted a photo of Amini's family members hugging one another in the deserted hospital corridor. They had just been told Mahsa was dead.

The image's impact was explosive. It remains seared into many Iranians' memories. Mahsa Amini had died five days short of her twenty-third birthday and without realizing her dream of becoming a doctor, but she was not forgotten by her nation. The Islamic Republic of Iran is a huge country, stretching from the green, snow-capped Caucasus Mountains in the north through arid desert to the Persian Gulf in the south. Its population is also large—roughly ninety million—and multi-ethnic. Amini's death unified the entire nation against the brutal, authoritarian regime that had taken her life. Even today, long after the nightly running skirmishes between protesters and riot police have stopped, the echoes and implications of Amini's death pose a unique threat to a regime that has ruled Iran with an iron grip for forty-six years.

Death to the Dictator

The day after her death, on September 17, 2022, a large crowd gathered for Amini's funeral in her hometown of Saqqez in Kurdistan Province. "I swear to God that when she [Mahsa] left home, her clothes were so appropriate," cried Amini's mother, Mojgan Eftekhari, hunched over her grave. "Her Islamic coat was down to her feet. And now you are here, buried under the ground. I will pour all your grave soil on my head. My dear, I would sacrifice myself for you anytime."[20]

At the funeral, it also became clear that Amini's death signified something more to many attendees than the tragic story of a young woman who paid the ultimate price for being in the wrong place at the wrong time. While her mother protested that Amini had been in compliance with the Islamic Republic's dress code, other women ripped off their headscarves, in direct defiance of those laws. Attendees, most of whom had come from across Kurdistan, mixed mourning for Amini with angry anti-government chants, including, "Death to the Dictator"—a reference to Ayatollah Khamenei, Iran's Supreme Leader since 1989.[21]

As the Amini funeral turned into a direct challenge to the government, the response of state security forces also intensified. Up to that point, the government had tried to head off anger and protest through a combination of obfuscation, official lies, and hollow-sounding regret over Amini's death. Despite the documented condition of her body in the hospital, the police denied beating Amini at any point during her arrest and issued a statement that Amini had suffered from pre-existing health conditions and likely died of a heart attack. Law enforcement even released doctored CCTV footage of an unidentified woman collapsing in the police station. Former President Ebrahim Raisi, who had initiated stricter enforcement of hijab rules since coming into office and perhaps sensed mounting outrage, publicly demanded an investigation into Amini's death.

At Amini's funeral, however, the regime's mask slipped off. Law enforcement fired tear gas and live ammunition at protesting attendees. One of the first demonstrators to die—and the first to be killed in Amini's hometown of Saqqez—was thirty-two-year-old Fereydoun Mahmudi. Despite the hundreds of witnesses, security services continued to deny their role in the violence. "I was told that they did not kill him, that he must have had an enemy, that no officer had opened fire, and no bullets were fired,"[22] said Sharmin Habibi, Mahmudi's wife.

In the face of violent repression, protests had spread to Sanandaj, the provincial capital with a population of more than 400,000, by the night of Amini's funeral. Soon thereafter, the demonstrations expanded to the rest of Kurdistan and then Iran at large. Within days, public rage over Amini's death stretched across at least 160 urban areas, ranging from Tehran and other cosmopolitan cities to rural towns in all of Iran's thirty-one provinces.[23] Every day, social media was filled with images of clashes between protesters and police, army, and the Basij plainclothes paramilitary forces. Across the country, posters of Supreme Leader Khamenei were torn off walls.

Angel Losada, the Spanish Ambassador to Iran at the time, described the atmosphere to me in the nation's capital over the weekend of September 17 and 18th. "I attended a dinner with other ambassadors in Tehran. When I went in my official car to the event, all the streets were full of protests. I was told that this happens every now and then, but this seemed much more serious and more political. People were outraged and in the streets." Losada, who had been posted in the country since 2021, said he realized then that "this was going to be a very serious event."[24]

On September 22, protesters in several cities, including Tehran, burned police stations and vehicles. On September 30, security forces killed sixty-six people, including children, in Zahedan, a dusty city of 600,000 people near the Afghanistan-Pakistan border. By early October, the protests began to reach a fever pitch. On October 8, students at Al-Zahra, a female-only public university in Tehran, shouted "Get lost" at President Raisi during his official visit and pulled off their headscarves. On October 9, protesters routed government security forces, driving them out of the Kurdish city of Sanandaj, near Amini's hometown. That same day, Tehran's large bazaars shut down, with many merchants and retailers joining protesters in a march. Later that day, a police station in Tehran was set on fire.

Simultaneously, an official state broadcast on live TV was hijacked by an Iranian hacktivist group who displayed images of Amini and three other women killed in protests, as well as Supreme Leader Khamenei surrounded by flames with the slogan, "The blood of our youth is on your hands." The following day, October 10, workers in the oil industry, accounting for nearly a quarter of Iran's GDP, demonstrated against the regime. The government minimized the significance of these protests as mere wage disputes, but employees were calling for much more than a raise. Cities key for oil production, including Abadan, sitting on the Iraqi border just 35 miles from Basra, participated in the now-nationwide calls of "Death to the Dictator."[25]

In November and December of 2022, Ambassador Losada traveled to Saqqez, Amini's hometown in the Kurdish northwest of Iran, on a mission to get a Spanish citizen released from jail. The impact of the revolution there was stark. "I remember there being snow there. All the women there were without a hijab. There was a general strike. Saqqez was a ghost city. They didn't even open up a hotel for us. There was tension in the air." As more and more of the country burst into outright revolt, the protesters rattled the government, perhaps more than they realized. "At the time," said Losada, "the government was frightened that the regime could fall."[26]

However, Ayatollah Khamenei stayed true to character, responding forcefully to the protesters calling for his death, with his most defiant warning to date: "That seedling is a mighty tree now and no one should dare think they can uproot it." In other words, the endurance of the Islamic Republic, born out of revolution in 1979, was now unstoppable, even inevitable. But his declaration also served as a recognition of the transition of the Mahsa Amini protests from a series of passionate protests to a sustained movement that posed a threat to the state. His words probably only fueled protesters' ambitions. Even as state repression stepped up, including imprisonment, torture, and executions, the demonstrations following Amini's death continued into mid-2023.

The circumstances of Mahsa's death were certainly tragic and unjust by any measure. She was not a politicized activist with any history of confronting the Islamic Republic, but a young woman who liked makeup, sport, and was on her way to becoming a doctor. In short, she was very easy for many people to identify with. Nonetheless, the protests following her death were clearly about more than just one innocent, young life stolen away. Why, in a country accustomed to little democracy, the oppression of women, and the violent repression of protest and speech, did the death of one ordinary woman lead to a massive popular movement that vocally rejected not just their nation's leadership, but the Islamic Republic itself?

CHAPTER 3
ZAN, ZENDEGI, AZADI

"Victory means establishing democracy, peace and human rights and ending tyranny...We will not back down."
–Narges Mohammadi, Nobel Peace Prize Laureate, 2022

Mahsa Amini's name quickly became a rallying cry within Iran and shorthand for the violent oppression of women around the world, but it was not the same name she was known by in her hometown. Her family used her Kurdish name, Jina. At the time of Mahsa's birth, however, Iran had only permitted Persian or Islamic names on birth certificates. As a result, Kurdish children grew up with two names, a familial Kurdish one, as well as an official Persian or Islamic version.

This prohibition on Kurdish names was just one symptom of the repression of the Kurds and other ethnic minority groups within Iran. References to a Kurdish state or homeland in historical chronicles date back centuries, but modern nationhood has been hard to achieve. The first half of the 20th century saw five short-lived Kurdish states. Nonetheless, Kurds have persisted in demanding rights, ranging from official recognition of their language, to semi-autonomy within Iran, to establishing their own country. Greater Kurdistan transcends national borders, including parts of Iran, Iraq, Turkey, and Syria, and Kurds have had distinct experiences in each country. Iraq is the country in which Kurds have achieved the greatest autonomy, including their own standing militia, the Peshmerga. Iraqi soldiers are not allowed to enter the Kurdish region in northern Iraq.

In neighboring Iran, Kurdish aspirations for greater political control have been consistently stymied since the late 20th century up to the present. Two months after the 1979 revolution, Kurds launched their own rebellion, which failed, resulting in 30,000 Kurdish deaths. Forty-six years later, Kurdish people are still persecuted. A Sunni minority in Shi'a–majority Iran, Kurds make up approximately 10 percent of Iran's total population, yet they constitute almost half of the country's political prisoners. So, it was unsurprising that Kurds were more likely to be targeted by regime authorities—and were the first in the line of fire when protests broke out. After Mahsa Amini, one of the first people to be killed in Iran was Farjad Darvishi, a twenty-three-year-old Kurdish man. He was shot dead by security forces on September 20, 2022, during anti-government protests near his village in Urmia.[27]

Given this history of political and cultural suppression, the fact that Amini became recognized around the world under her Persian, not Kurdish, name was painful for some Kurds. Speaking about the erasure of Mahsa Amini's Kurdish name, Jina, in global coverage of the protests, Iranian Kurdish filmmaker Beri Shalmashi said, "I felt like she died twice because no one really was mentioning her Kurdish name or her Kurdish background, which is so relevant."[28]

The Seven Countries of Iran

Mahsa Jina Amini's Kurdish identity added another political layer to the protests around her death at the hands of police in Tehran. While Kurdish efforts for recognition and self-determination are probably the highest profile struggle by a minority within Iran, existing ethnic divisions cleave Iran far beyond the Kurdish minority in Iran's northwest. Several other groups have aspirations for greater autonomy within Iran, and often suffer disproportionately. There are separatist movements in Iranian Azerbaijan, Sistan and Baluchistan, as well as Arabs in Khuzestan. In fact, the dominant ethnic group of Iran, Persians, only comprise 61 percent of the nation's population, although many Iranians may claim more than one identity. So, while Kurdistan was the center of some of the most pitched and violent protests following Amini's death, other minority regions were not far behind.

"The remarkable acts of resistance following Jina's [Mahsa's] funeral in Kurdistan built on decades of activism and resistance that up to 'Jina's [Mahsa's] uprising' were largely unnoticed by the Iranian center," said Dr. Farangis Ghaderi, a lecturer in Kurdish and Gender Studies at the University of Exeter. "Jina's murder sparked unprecedented solidarity among marginalized and oppressed peoples of Iran and offered an opportunity to reflect on their struggles, aspirations and erased histories...When Kurds protest an authoritarian regime that uses political and economic oppression, they are also crying out against the denial of their identity by the Iranian state through the erasure of their names, languages, cultures and histories."[29]

As protests intensified across regions with high concentrations of ethnic minorities, so did Iranian repression. Zahedan, the capital of Sistan and Baluchistan province that sits on the Pakistani border, became the site of intense weekly protests after Friday prayers at the Makki Mosque, the largest Sunni mosque in Iran. A local religious leader named Molavi Abdolhamid delivered fiery speeches both against the Iranian regime's brutality and the mandatory hijab. Two weeks after Amini's death, on September 30, 2022, Zahedan witnessed one of the deadliest days in the protest movement's history. Known as "Bloody Friday," more than ninety-five people, including women and children, were killed, and hundreds more wounded after security forces opened fire on people protesting the rape of a fifteen-year-old Baluchi girl by a police officer.

To add insult to fatal injuries, officials made no effort to track down perpetrators of the violence, despite the devastating casualty count. "The number of protesters and bystanders shot by Iran's security forces on 'Bloody Friday' was the largest killed in a single day during the protests, but no one has been arrested," said Tara Sepehri Far, a senior researcher at Human Rights Watch.[30]

Disproportionately high rates of Kurds, Baluchis, and other minorities also faced the death penalty for alleged crimes.[31] In one example, Hossein Ali Dil Baluch, a twenty-seven-year-old member of the Baluchi minority group, was secretly executed in the middle of the night after being arrested on spurious drug-related charges on October 19, 2022.[32] A year and three months later, on January 23, 2024, political prisoner Farhad Salimi, belonging to the Kurdish Sunni minority, was also arbitrarily put to death in Karaj, west of Tehran, after he had "confessed" to his crime of committing "corruption on Earth"—a confession reportedly obtained through torture, mock executions and sleep deprivation.[33]

Another technique used by the IRGC to stomp out the protests was to rally Persian nationalist support by raising the specter of an Iran stripped of its ethnic provinces. In one case, the IRGC published a map of Iran broken up into seven different countries.[34] Authorities also sought to exploit existing disagreements between various ethnic groups, such as disputes over water rights between Kurdistan and neighboring Southern Azerbaijan.[35]

However, the Mahsa protests were so powerful because, while the regime tapped into pre-existing grievances of ethnic minorities, resistance to the clerical establishment that materialized at Mahsa's funeral in Kurdistan transcended ethnic boundaries. Protesters were, in fact, fully aware that keeping together their coalition of minority groups and Persians was essential to their success. The week after Amini died, dissident Iranian rapper Toomaj Salehi, who belongs to the Bakhtiari ethnic group in Iran and whose parents had also been detained as political prisoners in his youth, wrote in an Instagram post: "Unity is the secret to our victory. We are all Iran's family."[36] During the protests, he continued to use his platform to foster unity among Iranians of different backgrounds.[37]

Jin, Jiyan, Azadi

On September 17, 2022, thousands of people gathered in silence for Mahsa's public burial in Aychi cemetery, a cluster of gravestones and green trees in the midst of rolling yellow mountains.[38] Afterwards, the massive funeral procession of hundreds of cars choking the roads outside of Amini's Kurdish hometown of Saqqez turned into a protest, with mourners chanting three powerful Kurdish words forever etched into Iran's history: *Jin, Jiyan, Azadi* ("Woman, Life, Freedom").

The slogan was first popularized by the Kurdistan Workers' Party (PKK), a Kurdish secessionist, anti-capitalist, anti-patriarchal organization, shortly after it was founded by Abdullah Öcalan in 1978, who argued that national liberation begins with the liberation of women, coining the maxim: "A country can't be free unless all women are free." As a result of its guerilla attacks against the Turkish state, the PKK was designated a terrorist organization by the United States in 1997 and the European Union in 2004, and served as a manifestation of the ayatollah's worst nightmare: Kurdish independence *and* female emancipation.

Following the teachings of Öcalan, female Kurdish activists and fighters sprouted in the 1990s across Syria, Turkey and Iran. In Turkey especially, these fighters helped facilitate the rise of female activists and politicians in non-violent branches of the Kurdish movement in Turkey. The PKK's legacy is one reason why Kurdish political parties tend to have high rates of female representation in leadership positions in Turkish politics.[39]

Even before Amini's death, the slogan became so famous internationally that Europeans began adopting their own English version of the Kurdish slogan to demand an end to violence against women globally, including in their home countries.[40] On November 25, 2015, as women gathered to mark the annual International Day for the Elimination of Violence Against Women, demonstrators chanted "Woman, Life, Freedom" in cities across Europe, from Rotterdam, Gothenburg and Helsinki to Frankfurt and Essen.[41]

At the 2018 Cannes Film Festival, the actors and actresses in *Girls of the Sun,* a film about a Kurdish female battalion defending its villages from ISIS forces in Syria and Iraq, chanted *"Jin, Jiyan, Azadi."* Iranian-French lead actress Golshifteh Farahani had long fought for women's rights. In early 2009, she was forced into exile in Paris after being sentenced to death in Iran for posing in the nude around the time she starred in the Hollywood thriller "Body of Lies," alongside Leonardo DiCaprio and Russell Crowe.

Returning to Iran was not an option for Farahani. Three years later, in January 2012, Farahani's parents received a phone call at their apartment in Tehran from a man claiming to work at the Supreme Court of the Islamic Republic. Golshifteh would be punished severely for her on-screen immodesty, the official warned, adding that the film star's breast would be cut off and presented to her parents on a plate.[42] Asked what "*Jin, Jiyan, Azadi*" means to her, Farahani later said: "For women, freedom is a hope. It is women who march toward a life full of freedom…I wish freedom and peace upon all the Kurdish people."[43]

Following Amini's death, the slogan spread across Iran, becoming perhaps the most prominent example of Kurdish resistance being adopted by the nation as a whole. From Tehran to small regional cities, protesters adopted the slogan of the Kurdish women who had fought against the Islamic State in Syria, chanting "Zan, Zendegi, Azadi"—the Persian Translation of "Jin, Jiyan, Azadi."

As footage of Mahsa's funeral spread online, thousands of women took to the streets to protest, staging the boldest acts of civil disobedience Iran has seen since 1979. Some ripped off their hijabs. Others set their head scarves on fire in open defiance of the regime to signal that they could no longer be controlled in their daily lives. Forty days after her death—a significant commemorative milestone in Islam marking the formal ending of the mourning period—protests at the graveyard where Amini was buried produced one of the most viral images of the protests: a woman atop a car with her long hair running freely down her back. Under the Islamic Republic, not wearing hijab was itself an act of revolution. As significant as the multi-ethnic coalition was to the rapid and intense spread of the Mahsa protests, the single biggest driving factor was a shared experience under the Islamic Republic: the repression of women.

"We Did Not Have a Revolution To Go Backwards"

The word "hijab" came to Persian from the Arabic word meaning "to conceal," and has been a contentious political issue for centuries in Iran. By 1848, the custom of women covering their neck and hair as a form of modesty—often wearing the long fabric *chador*—had been widespread in Iran for hundreds of years. However, that year is remembered for the radical actions of an erudite poet, scholar and prodigious women's activist named Fatimah Baraghani, who delivered a sermon with her hair uncovered in front of an audience of men.⁴⁴ Baraghani, also known as *Qurrrat al-'Ayn* ("comfort of the eyes") and *Tahirih/Tahira* ("pure") so shocked the audience that, in an apocryphal account, one man slit his throat at the horror of seeing a woman's hair unveiled. The swift and harsh punishment for her actions was very real. Baraghani was thrown into jail and executed by strangulation for her brazen actions.

A few decades later, under the rule of Reza Shah, the requirement and cultural expectation of wearing hijab began to fade. In 1926, the Shah offered military protection for any woman who wished to go without a *chador* in public. Ten years later, in 1936, the Shah criminalized the hijab as part of his drive to modernize the country along Western, secular lines. In addition to female head coverings, the ban extended to the wearing of some traditional men's clothing. The edict was enforced by police who were instructed to remove head coverings from women seen wearing them in public—a somewhat inverted *Gasht-e Ershad*, or morality police.

Unsurprisingly, the Shah's decree was controversial and resisted by Islamic clerics and devout Muslims. Five years later, the Shah abdicated the throne. While his successor maintained a less punitive environment toward the hijab, women were nonetheless strongly encouraged not to wear head coverings, particularly in professional settings. This modern approach to women's rights also included formally enfranchising women in 1963, following many Western nations, but eight years ahead of Switzerland, where women did not gain the right to participate in national elections until 1971.

This atmosphere of tolerance quickly changed following the 1979 Iranian revolution and establishment of the Islamic Republic. Though the revolution was fueled by a coalition of groups disillusioned with the rule of Mohammad Reza Pahlavi, many of which were not particularly religious, it quickly evolved into a dictatorship that used its strict interpretation of Sharia law to restrict diversity, democracy, freedom and the rights of women. In a matter of a few years, abortion was criminalized, women lost the right to a divorce from their spouse, and the hijab became mandatory.

One of the early signals that women's rights were going to go backwards under Ayatollah Khomeini's Iran was the annulment of the Family

Protection Act in 1979. The law, which the Shah's government had instituted in 1975, gave women basic rights common in Western countries around divorce and abortion. However, Khomeini saw the law as particularly offensive to the kind of theocracy he had envisaged. Men were granted full rights in divorce and custody, restrictions on polygamy were relaxed and the legal age of marriage for girls was lowered from eighteen to nine.

Iranian women were just as quick to resist the fundamentalist turn of the revolution. On March 4, 1979, the daily conservative newspaper *Kayhan* published an editorial with the headline: "Let's Not Forget the Women," which questioned why, among the legacy of the Shah's policies, should the Family Protection Act be singled out.[45] On March 8, 1979, International Women's Day, just weeks after the revolution, tens of thousands of women flooded the streets of Tehran to protest against the forced veiling of women. Crowds chanted "We did not have a revolution to go backwards."

Among those joining the protest was Kate Millett, an American feminist writer and educator. She had traveled to Tehran to support the women of Iran in their demands for gender equality. Even women who wore the veil of their own accord protested, insisting on the centrality of choice. When one reporter asked Millett on air what she thought of Khomeini and his nascent religious state, she looked straight into the camera and described the Supreme Leader as a "male chauvinist pig."[46]

Millett's gripe was not with Islamic clothing customs but with the absence of choice and the attempts to force women to accept second-class status. Speaking later to the *Washington Post*,[47] Millett recounted two things that "astonished" her when she first arrived in Tehran in 1979: "There was a wall of women in *chadors*. It was enormously dramatic and beautiful—a kind of theater. I think the *chador* is a beautiful garment if you wear it by choice, rather than forced on pain of being spat on or stoned or threatened with one's life. It's a bit like long skirts—I love to wear them, but you can't do any work in a *chador* or carry anything and that veil is telling you you are no one. Physically, it's like bound feet." [The second thing Millett noticed was] "the guns...then I realized I was here. A naked carbine is as oppressive as hell. In one second, my eyes swept the wall of black figures and right behind them was a gun in the hands of a very nervous youth, his finger on the trigger." Millett was later arrested for her activism and kicked out of the country.

Later in 1979, the crusading Italian journalist Oriana Fallaci interviewed Ayatollah Khomeini, who again elucidated his stance on the hijab, instructing women to conceal their bodies and hair so as not to attract men or boys. "If this piece of clothing did not exist—the Islamic dress— women could not work in a useful and healthy way. And not even men."[48] Later in the contentious interview, Khomeini made clear that he didn't care if Fallaci followed Islamic rules of dress because it was "for good and proper young women." Fallaci promptly removed her *chador* and continued the interview.[49]

Khomeini's infamous "Little Green Book," a compilation of Islamic decrees, also illuminated precisely how the country's new leader regarded women. His list of the "things which are impure" included urine, excrement, sperm, bones, blood, dogs, pigs, non-Muslim men, and women, wine, beer and the "sweat of the excrement-eating camel."[50]

While Fallaci was able to leave the country safely, Iranian women who resisted the Islamic Republic's new requirements around female dress and behavior often faced imprisonment and violence. On May 8, 1980, Farrokhru Parsa, the first female cabinet minister in Iran and one of the most vocal advocates for gender equality, was hanged after being charged with corruption in a kangaroo court. Parsa, who had served as Iran's minister of education from 1968 to 1977, was sentenced to death for "wasting and plundering public properties, propagating corruption and prostitution in the domain of culture, appointing pervert individuals to important ministry positions, organizing mixed outdoor camps and violating Islamic morality."[51]

Though it wouldn't save her life, Parsa's tenacity was on show right until the bitter end. Author Mansoureh Pirnia described Parsa's final moments alive in *Mrs. Minister:* "They put her in a sack, wrapped ropes around her and dragged her to the gallows. The ropes were torn. Once she regained consciousness, she was once again taken to the gallows, but this time they wrapped wires around her. Apparently, she hadn't died the second time either. The three holes in the dead body of one of the most influential Iranian women is a testimony of her most painful death."

Four years after the Islamic Revolution, on August 9, 1983, the mandatory hijab was officially incorporated in the Islamic Penal Code passed by the Iranian parliament, or *majlis*: "Women who appear in public places and thoroughfares without observing the Islamic hijab shall be sentenced to imprisonment from ten days to two months or fined."[52] Khomeini's war on what he considered one of the most corrupting insults to Islam, women's bodily autonomy, was well underway. And, as Amini's detainment tragically demonstrated forty years later, the punishment for improper hijab was sometimes much worse.

Women Walking a Tightrope

The role of women in post-1979 Iran has been severely constricted by the Islamic Republic's interpretation of Islamic law, yet women have found ways to thrive and rise above the unrelenting oppression. For example, in 2022 women in Iran had a literacy rate of nearly 99 percent. This level represents not only a doubling of pre-1979 Revolution female literacy—in 1976, literacy among Iranian women was a little over 42 percent—but is well above the global average of 87 percent.[53] Women, like Amini, have access to graduate-level education. Politically, women are elected to the *majlis* and frequently serve in the president's cabinet. But all of these successes are hard-won examples of women pushing through a labyrinth of barriers put in their way to excel academically and professionally. In 2025, Iran remains a complicated, difficult, and at times harrowing place for women to navigate. Take, for example, the story of the young female CEO Maryam Banihashemi.

Banihashemi was one of the millions of successful Iranian professional women. At one point, her firm, Avantegarde Company, oversaw fifty employees and had an important relationship with elements of Iran's regular army, Artesh, on projects spanning petrochemical, oil, and fast-moving consumer goods (FMCG). Banihashemi, who was CEO at the age of 30, was in charge of managing relationships with major corporations including

Renault and MAPNA, one of Iran's largest industrial conglomerates. As part of her job, she also had to contend with retired members of the Artesh, some of whom had also been commanders at the IRGC. These powerful, well-connected men often employed aggressive corporate tactics in order to monopolize and control Iranian industries. "After two years working with Artesh, they pushed us to be partners," Banihashemi told me in mid-2024. "That's what they do. They go after start-ups with innovative ideas and force them into a partnership or to sell parts of their shares. That's how they control the markets."

As the pressure campaign continued, Banihashemi also increasingly found herself in uncomfortable personal encounters with retired military commanders, first in the office and then after hours. She started receiving text messages from an anonymous number that she later found out had been a "seventy-year-old" military general now serving as a senior manager at her firm.

The general invited Banihashemi to be his temporary wife in an arrangement known as a *sigheh,* where a man and women enter into a contract for a specified period of time that enables them to engage in sexual relations. A *sigheh* can be terminated without an onerous legal divorce and a man is not financially obligated to support a woman in this temporary marriage framework.[54] Less generous interpretations of *sigheh* see it as sanctimonious prostitution.

Banihashemi herself was repulsed by the seventy-year-old general's proposition, describing the encounter as wildly inappropriate and "disgusting." She added that this was a loophole through which men could have extra-marital relationships with Islamic cover. "I couldn't say yes because then I would be selling myself," she said. However, the unequal power dynamics in their relationship also threatened the business she had built. "If I said no, he wouldn't let me manage projects and withheld money I needed to pay my employees," said Banihashemi.

So, when those lewd texts lit up her phone, Banihashemi faced an impossible dilemma. "It's common for women around the world to feel pressure," Banihashemi added. "But in Iran, harassment is normalized."[55] By 2015, she had reached a breaking point and tendered her resignation, knowing that doing so also meant she would have to leave Iran. Fortunately, she was able to join her German-Iranian boyfriend in Dusseldorf, later relocating to Zurich when he got a job at Google.

In recent years, Banihashemi has emerged as the face of the Iranian women's movement in Switzerland, where she works as a strategic consultant for various NGOs and has been vocal in calling for regime change in Iran. "After Mahsa's death, I was 200 percent focused on the 'Woman, Life, Freedom' movement," she said, noting that she continues to receive endless death threats on social media. "But in the West, there still isn't enough of a political willingness to bring about change in Iran. The international community should offer real support, not just talking and political gesturing. They should actively end dialog, financial support and opportunities granted to the Islamic Republic."

Veil Wars

Though Banihashemi is a high-profile international advocate for women's rights in Iran, ordinary women—and men—inside the nation have continued to resist the Islamic Republic's imposition of the mandatory veil ever since 1979. In 2006, the women-led One Million Signatures Campaign[56] delivered a petition to the *majlis* to end legal discrimination against women. Their demands included:

- Equal rights for women in marriage and divorce
- An end to polygamy and temporary marriages (*mut'ah*)
- An increase in the age of criminal responsibility to 18 for both boys and girls
- Equal inheritance rights for men and women
- Equal compensation for bodily injury or death for men and women
- Equal legal testimony rights for men and women

Eight years later, in 2014, Masih Alinejad, an Iranian-American human rights activist and journalist in New York opposed to the mandatory hijab, launched a Facebook campaign called "My Stealthy Freedom" to document images of thousands of unveiled Iranian women inside the country.

Three years later, in 2017, Alinejad launched a new social media campaign called "#WhiteWednesdays," encouraging thousands of women across Iran to post photos and videos of themselves either wearing white headscarves and articles of clothing as a symbol of protest or capturing footage of the regime's sometimes-violent hijab enforcement methods.[57]

Men created memorable campaigns of their own. Some posted photos of themselves wearing a skirt and hijab in solidarity with their female compatriots. In 2016, the hashtag #meninhijab went viral showing images of men, somewhat mockingly, adhering to the country's mandatory hijab laws. That trend continued during the Mahsa Amini protests as veiled men were filmed walking the streets and manning storefronts dressed in female garb.[58]

Years before Mahsa Amini's death, women had already been resisting state-enforced mandatory hijab laws. On December 27, 2017, thirty-two-year-old Vida Movahed staged a silent, but memorable protest. Vida climbed atop an electrical utility box five-feet high on Enqelab ("Revolution") Street, a bustling commercial street in central Tehran, removed her white headscarf, tied it to a long stick and started waving it, letting her long brunette hair flow freely. She stood up on that platform, alone, for an hour. The somber act of defiance was captured on camera and spread like wildfire. She was subsequently arrested, found guilty of inciting public "corruption," and briefly jailed for her actions.

However, Movahed's silent defiance struck a chord with Iranian women. Authorities went on to issue twenty-nine additional arrests of women on similar charges the following year, including Narges Hosseini, then thirty-one-years-old, who on January 29, 2018, was filmed climbing onto that same utility box and waving a white flag to protest the mandatory hijab, earning the moniker of the 'Second Girl of Revolution Street.'

Soon, women and men started to mimic this form of civil disobedience across the country, including Azam Jangravi and Maryam Shariatmadari, setting off a short-lived movement that came to be known as the "Girls of

Enqelab Revolution," with the hashtag "#GirlsOfRevolutionSt" proliferating on social media networks.

In early 2019, two Tehrani women were arrested by the morality police for waving white scarves in defiance of the mandatory hijab. They were forced into a van to be taken to a detention center. But crowds, fed up with the treatment of women, surrounded the van, ripping off the van's door and setting the women free.[59] The Mahsa Amini protests, while unprecedented in scope and longevity, came after years of anti-hijab movements in Iran, as well as violent state repression.

By 2019, the scattered protests intensified and Ayatollah Khamenei resorted to subduing demonstrators through blunt force, setting in motion the bloodiest crackdown on Iranian protesters since the 1979 Islamic Revolution.[60] In less than two weeks in mid-November 2019, around 1,500 people were killed by Iran's security forces in what later came to be known as "Bloody November."

Of course, these determined protests have not shifted the stance of today's clerical establishment. Ayatollah Ali Khamenei, who succeeded Khomeini as *rahbar* (leader) following his death in 1989, continues to espouse the foundational precepts of the Islamic Republic. In fact, under the presidency of Ebrahim Raisi, Iranian state forces confronted demands for women's rights by doubling down on repression. In August 2022, a month before Mahsa Amini's death, Raisi said, "In the history of Islamic Iran, the life of the women of Iran has always been associated with chastity and the hijab."[61]

By that point, Raisi had initiated policies designed to squelch resistance to strict hijab seen on the streets of Tehran and other cities, where women were wearing their head coverings more loosely, with more hair visible. The former president—whose election had been backed by Khamenei and other conservative Islamic clerics and dogged by claims of election fraud—ordered a crackdown with more severe enforcement of laws by the morality police. In so doing, Raisi created a climate of confrontational suppression that galvanized the actions of the morality police who arrested Amini in mid-September.

In addition to ripping off their veils, Iranian women embraced another form of protest. In Iran, the act of cutting one's hair is a sign of mourning. The practice was first invoked more than one thousand years ago by the poet Ferdowsi in the Iranian national epic, the Shahnameh (Book of Kings), written between 977 and 1010 CE. Believed to be the longest poem ever written by a single author, the Shahnameh cites *Gisuboran*, or cutting hair, as an act of mourning when the hero Siyavash is executed and his wife, Farangis, cuts her hair to protest the injustice. The same practice is observed by Kurds and Bakhtiari groups.

After Amini's death, the significance of cutting one's hair expanded into an act of protest, a contagious act of bravery. Thousands of Iranian women cut off locks of hair to mourn not just Amini, but also the degeneration of their country. For decades, hair had been exploited by the Islamic Republic as a weapon of discrimination and harassment against women, imposing arcane restrictions over their bodies. Now women were wresting back control. They were cutting off the very hair that had been used to control them in the first place.

Thousands more women abroad followed suit in a sign of solidarity. Among them was Darya Safai, an Iranian-born politician and member of the Belgian parliament. When I talked to Safai, she explained that she and her husband had organized student protests in 1999, but fled their native country after their apartment was ransacked and Safai was briefly detained by police. In October of 2022, Safai, along with two other lawmakers, cut their hair in the Belgian parliament.[62] "Mahsa Amini was the same age as my daughter," Safai later said over a WhatsApp call. "When we buried Mahsa in Iran in 2022, we knew we couldn't let her go for nothing. That was the point where we were going to take a stand, because this regime not only took our hair—the ayatollahs also took away our freedom and dignity."[63]

A more idiosyncratic symbol of solidarity appeared that month when AleXsandro Palombo, an Italian artist, painted a striking image on the wall of Iran's consulate in Milan—a cartoon of Marge Simpson with her towering blue hair cut off in solidarity with the protesters in Iran.[64]

While the Mahsa Amini street protests had largely subsided by mid-2023, the legacy of civil disobedience has persisted. Restrictive rules of modesty for women remain in place in Iran in 2025, but more women than ever are defying the regime and walking in public with their hair unveiled, in large part because of the Mahsa Amini protest movement.

Leading Women

Controlling a divided and fragmented nation is a much simpler proposition than containing a united people. The protesters who took to the streets and social media in 2022 and 2023 were different in political leanings, socio-economic backgrounds, faiths, ethnicities, professions, genders and ages, but they were bound by a shared desire to topple a tyranny that they believed was depriving them, particularly women, of fundamental liberties. The explosive anger directed at the Islamic Republic starting in the fall of 2022 had roots in the long-standing struggles for equality among different ethnic groups. Despite their differences, the varied ethnic groups overcame these gulfs in a way that allowed the Mahsa Amini protests to be more impactful and disruptive than they could have been had these differences divided them.

As it turned out, the Kurdish slogan *Jin, Jiyan, Azadi*, once easily translated to the Persian *Zan, Zendegi, Azadi*, served as a battlecry for Iranians worldwide. The chant tapped into a pent-up anger toward a brutal, corrupt regime in a way that transcended ethnic divisions. It succinctly encapsulated the feelings, particularly held among younger Iranians, toward a government that trampled on their country's environment, mismanaged the economy, enriched the clerical elite, isolated the country further away from the international community, and aligned itself with other authoritarian regimes in Russia, China and North Korea.

But the most important word in that slogan was the first, *Jin* or *Zan*. The protest had been sparked by the death of a woman, led by many others, and embraced female emancipation from mandatory, strict adherence to religious law that relegated women to second-class status and beat them into submission. "Death to the Dictator" is easier to yell at protests, but the anger on the streets was prompted by a system that granted women far fewer rights than men in marriage, divorce, child custody and legal inheritance. In putting female emancipation at the center of their demonstrations, the protesters were targeting one of the core values underpinning the conservative clerical establishment. For Supreme Leader Khamenei, bolstering women's rights was tantamount to waging an existential war on the Islamic Republic.

CHAPTER 4
A CULTURE OF PROTEST:
FROM CROWN TO TURBAN

"The social order destroyed by a revolution is almost always better than that which immediately preceded it, and experience shows that the most dangerous moment for a bad government is generally that in which it sets about reform."
–Alexis de Tocqueville, French political theorist, historian and politician, 1856

When U.S. President Jimmy Carter visited Iran in late December of 1977, he delivered what turned out to be one of the least prophetic pronouncements of the twentieth century. At an extravagant New Year's Eve state dinner hosted by Shah Mohammad Reza Pahlavi, Carter described Iran, then a staunch U.S. ally, as an "island of stability in one of the more troubled areas of the world." The celebration was held in Tehran's Niavaran Complex, a series of large buildings and palaces dating back to the 1700s. In that tightly-controlled bubble created by Pahlavi's wealth and almost four decades of iron-fisted rule, Carter's words might have rung true. But the situation elsewhere in the country was far from tranquil. A revolution was brewing that would turn Iran into one of the most tumultuous countries on the planet.

Within a year of Carter's speech, nationwide unrest would paralyze the country, forcing Pahlavi to flee Iran for Egypt and then later to the United States for specialized treatment for lymphatic cancer that would go on to kill him in July 1980. Before the Shah's death, though, Ayatollah Khomeini's theocratic government had begun consolidating power in Iran. In fact, it was less than two years after Carter's speech, on November 4, 1979, that the U.S. Embassy in Tehran was overrun by Islamic revolutionaries who held more than fifty Americans hostage for 444 days. The prolonged hostage crisis ended up being a stain on Carter's presidency, likely playing a role in his failed re-election bid against Ronald Reagan. Iran freed the hostages the same day Reagan was sworn in as the country's fortieth president, January 20, 1981, but the two countries have never re-established diplomatic relationships.

History of Tumult

The 1979 revolution was the most successful uprising in modern Iranian history, particularly in terms of longevity. However, it was far from the first popular revolt in Iran. In the early twentieth century, for example, young revolutionaries who were disillusioned by the then-ruling Qajar dynasty's spiraling corruption, unchecked opulence, and foreign influence, banded together with intellectuals and progressive clerics to create the first grassroots movement of its kind in the Middle East to challenge the authority of the Shah. The resulting Constitutional Revolution of 1905 demanded the formation of an elected parliament (*majlis*) and constitution to create what would be, essentially, a parliamentary democracy governed by rule of law that sought to democratize education and institute constitutional limitations on power.

A 1921 revolt, also known as the "Persian Coup D'état," that led to several years of political upheaval eventually ended the Qajar dynasty after over 130 years of rule. However, that reign was not replaced by a constitutional state, but by a military officer named Reza Shah Pahlavi who ruled with no meaningful constitutional checks on his power. Following World War II—another period of political tumult that included an Anglo-Soviet invasion of Iran in August 1941—Pahlavi's son, Mohammad Reza Pahlavi, was named the head of state. Finally, Iran formally had a constitutional monarchy, although in practice the *majlis* was relatively weak and unstable. In 1952, Pahlavi alleviated further restraints on his power by ejecting Prime Minister Mohammed Mossadegh from office.

Mossadegh had emerged as a popular leader hoping to nationalize the country's oil industry as a means of taking back control over Iran's key natural resources from the grip of the UK, the U.S., and other international parties. Pahlavi's decision to remove Mossadegh, encouraged by Western nations, led to another significant insurgency. As a result, Pahlavi reinstated Mossadegh as Prime Minister. But, following Mossadegh's return as premier, the U.S. and the UK, still alarmed by his nationalization plans, plotted with disillusioned Iranian aristocrats and bureaucrats to successfully orchestrate a covert operation in 1953, dubbed "Operation Ajax," to stir mass unrest inside Iran, unseat Mossadegh, and eventually restore the country's pro-Western Pahlavi monarchy. Mossadegh was arrested and confined to his home until his death in 1967, after which he was interred in his living room, despite his wish to be buried in a public graveyard alongside victims of political persecution.[65] This Western interference in Iranian politics was not soon forgotten by Iranians. In fact, it was cited a quarter century later by Khomeinists as evidence that Pahlavi lacked the political legitimacy and mandate from the people of Iran to stay in power.

Following Mossadegh's arrest, Pahlavi remained in power for nearly three more decades, but his authoritarian rule fanned discontent among different segments of the population. While women enjoyed more freedoms under the Pahlavi dynasty than under the previous Qajars or the subsequent Islamic Republic, social and political protests were still subject to surveillance and harassment by SAVAK, the Shah's secret and dreaded intelligence service formed in 1957. The lack of freedoms and perception of a corrupt Shah led to numerous popular uprisings. Among the largest followed the arrest of cleric Ayatollah Ruhollah Khomeini—the future Supreme Leader of Iran—in the early 1960s, which set off massive popular demonstrations and rioting around the country. In the 1970s, a radical left-wing group, Mujahedin-e-Khalq (MEK), fought an ongoing guerilla war against the Shah. These repeated protests targeting the social and political order are a somewhat rare continuity between pre- and post-1979 Iranian politics.

The Pahlavi Party Ends

By 1978, the massive discontent over the authoritarian rule of the Shah brought together multiple otherwise opposed elements in Iranian society in the most successful popular uprising in modern Iran. Led by the formerly exiled Ruhollah Khomeini, the revolutionary coalition that ultimately unseated the Shah represented an unprecedented mobilization of the masses, from conservative Islamic clerics to leftist MEK guerillas. Khomeini unified these elements by playing to widespread Iranian discontent about the incumbent Pahlavi monarchy that had for too long flaunted its opulent way of life at the expense of its own people.

A lavish, three-day party that Mohammad Reza Pahlavi hosted in October 1971 to commemorate the 2,500th anniversary of the Persian Empire is often cited as proof of the monarchy's detachment from the dreary reality of ordinary Iranians. The celebrations that the Shah planned would be "the most wonderful thing the world has ever seen," consisting of an unforgettable display of decadent pageantry that he said would "reawaken the people of Iran to their past and reawaken the world to Iran."[66]

Preparations for the party included building an intricately designed tent city in Persepolis, fortified with bulletproof windows to protect the high-level guests, and 20 miles of silk weaving through the dozens of luxury prefabricated apartments erected for the multi-day banquet. Fifteen hundred Cypress trees, 50,000 carnations and another 50,000 songbirds were imported for the majestic aesthetic. Eighteen tons of food was flown in from Paris, including roast peacock and quail eggs, for the 600 invitees hailing from sixty-three countries. Officials from the royal court were dressed in exquisite attire from French luxury fashion house Lanvin. Guests included Ethiopian emperor Haile Selassie and the kings and queens of Belgium, Denmark, Norway, Jordan and Nepal, along with the presidents of Pakistan, Turkey, Romania and Russia, who were chauffeured to and from the airport in 250 ultra-luxury red Mercedes-Benz 600 limousines. The total cost for the party was estimated to be in the hundreds of millions of dollars. Sensitive to potential backlash about the ostentation of the celebrations, Queen Farah Diba Pahlavi told her planning committee that the idea behind the Persepolis party was "to prove that the times we are living in now, the Pahlavi era, is a period of renaissance for Iranian civilization."[67]

As the Shah was throwing the most expensive party in modern history for more than sixty royals and heads of state in the ruins of Persepolis, vast swathes of the country's population were living in despair. Many Iranians lacked access to potable water, education, and basic medicine. The event, set out to celebrate the Shah's heritage and enduring legacy, ended up hastening the monarchy's downfall, with the Islamic Revolution ejecting him from power eight years later.

From his place of exile in Najaf, Iraq, during the weeklong October 1971 Persepolis celebrations, Ruhollah Khomeini, for the first time, called for the downfall of the Persian monarchy and for the installation to power of an institution focused on the betterment of everyday Iranians. "One should commemorate a rule that uses the sword to protect its people and protect them from fear," Khomeini said. "But as for a regime founded on oppression and thievery whose only aim is to satisfy its own lustful desire—only when it is overthrown can the people celebrate and rejoice."[68]

The promise of a brighter future and greater freedoms was attractive to many Iranians when Khomeini's revolutionary movement started to gather momentum in 1978. After all, Khomeini had pledged that, following a successful revolution, he would relinquish the reins of power to the country's elected representatives and would leave politics altogether, retiring to the holy city of Qom. In September 1978, speaking from exile in Paris, Khomeini said, "Our intention is not that religious leaders should themselves administer the state, but that they should guide the people in determining what the demands of Islam are."[69] Khomeini's manifesto, which sought to remove the Shah from power, attracted a mass uprising unparalleled in size and demographic scope in modern Iranian history, even though it long predated the organizing capabilities of social media.

"When the revolution took place, I was sixteen," recalled Parastou Forouhar, an installation artist based in Germany who was born and raised in Iran to parents who she said fought for democracy throughout their lives and were later murdered by Islamic Republic agents in Tehran in the 1990s. "Intellectuals, liberals, democrats, people like my parents, committed themselves to the revolution," said Forouhar, "but the religious forces gained the upper hand. The Islamic Republic grew into a monster that uses tradition and religion to oppose diversity, freedom, democracy and the rights of women. And enforces its rule with brutality."[70]

From Shah to Supreme Leader

The revolution that ensued in 1979, among the first to be televised worldwide, remains the defining moment in Iran's recent history, dramatically transforming the country's relationship with the rest of the world. Khomeinists were staunchly anti-Western and anti-liberal. They rejected growing U.S. encroachment in the Middle East, free markets, as well as the legitimacy of the State of Israel to exist as a sovereign nation. "Death to America" and "Death to Israel" served as core guiding principles for the burgeoning theocracy.

"Our final victory will come when all foreigners are out of the country," Khomeini said on February 1, 1979 to 1,200 of his supporters after he landed in Tehran's Mehrabad Airport in a chartered Air France 747 airliner from Paris. "I beg God to cut off the hands of all evil foreigners and their helpers."[71]

That day, Khomeini's millions of followers who lined the streets of Tehran to greet him saw a full-blown revolution as an avenue that would herald attractive opportunities—more social and political freedoms, a more equitable economy, and independence from foreign powers.

In a sense, the prospect of a revolution was a sort of Rorschach test in which people with different backgrounds and ambitions for Iran could project their best hopes and dreams onto the movement. There were, however, clues as to the ultimate direction that a Khomeini-led revolution might take. For example, broadsheets in Iran reported on the Shah's departure from the country after a year of mass protests against his rule with headlines like "*Shah raft*" ("The Shah has Gone") and published new headlines about Khomeini's historic return: "*Imam amad*" ("The Spiritual

Leader has arrived"). In Shia Islam, the position of *Imam* is a vaunted one, just one rung below the Prophet Muhammad. By February 12, 1979, Khomeini's status had been elevated to that of a near god-like figure. As it turned out, Khomeini forgot his vow to leave politics to the professionals following the revolution. Instead, he became the country's Supreme Leader and ruled for a decade with God-like impunity.

Another hint of what kind of government Khomeini envisioned can be gleaned from his 1970 book, *Islamic Government*, a compilation of his lectures, also known as the "Little Green Book." In it, Khomeini contends that the country's Shi'a clergy (*ulama*) are the most fitting custodians and administrators of state power until the return of the Hidden Imam, a messianic figure in Shi'a lore.[72]

As a post-revolution political system emerged, Khomeini began steering the country toward a form of government that was every bit as authoritarian as the Shah who had just been forced from the country. The "Little Green Book" ended up serving as the theoretical underpinning on which the Islamic Republic of Iran was founded. Khomeinist thought deviated from other Islamic governments in that, rather than clerics having responsibility to interpret Sharia law in the court system, they would also control other traditionally secular functions of government.

The centrality of conservative *sharia* law also ensured that the new regime would, in many cases, be directly opposed to the modernizing Western influences of the Pahlavi era, dominated by the Shia clergy, and heavily influenced by their interpretation of the teachings of the Prophet Muhammad. In October 1979, a new constitution was ratified, cementing Khomeini's religious and political supremacy over Iran through the doctrine of *velayat-e faqih* (guardianship of the Islamic jurist), ensuring that the rule of the clergy superseded that of the state.

The rapid emergence of an authoritarian Islamic Republic led by a Supreme Leader—a system of government diametrically opposed to the hopes of many Iranians—shocked many people who supported the revolution. The story of the Shah's last Prime Minister, Shapour Bakhtiar, was emblematic of the dramatic shift in power that began in 1979. As anti-Pahlavi sentiment grew, Bakhtiar convinced the Shah to leave the country, perhaps thinking that he would be better able to manage mounting discontent with Pahlavi out of the country. Soon thereafter, Bakhtiar himself began losing authority and power to the ascending Khomeinist movement. His tenure as Prime Minister lasted just thirty-eight days after the country's military withdrew its support, forcing Bakhtiar to flee the country himself.[73]

From Paris, Bakhtiar went on to become a leading critic of the Islamic Republic and a fervent constitutional monarchist. In August 1980, along with other Iranian dissidents, he founded the National Movement of Iranian Resistance (NAMIR). NAMIR's mission was to "establish the rule of law in Iran under a political system whose form and principles shall be freely approved and elected by the Iranian nation within the framework of international law."[74]

However, even in Western Europe, Bakhtiar was not safe from the wrath of Iran's new leadership. Within a year of its founding, the Islamic Republic expanded its mission from eliminating foreign influence to silencing dissidents *outside* Iran. On July 18, 1980, French police foiled an assassination attempt on Bakhtiar.[75] However, eleven years later, on August 6, 1991, the former Prime Minister was found strangled and stabbed to death in his home in the Parisian suburb of Suresnes.

"From Iranian Revolution to Islamic Revolution"

Bakhtiar was not the only prominent leader who misjudged Khomeini's intentions. Abolhassan Bani-Sadr, who in 1980 was elected as the first President of the Islamic Republic of Iran, claimed that Khomeini betrayed him by leading him to believe that clerical leaders driving change were doing so in the interest of heralding a new era of democracy and human rights in a post-Pahlavi Iran. "When he was in [exile in] France, he was on the side of freedom," an eighty-five-year-old Bani-Sadr reflected in 2019 at his home in Versailles, outside Paris, where he lived since fleeing from Iran in 1981 until his death in late 2021. "It was when he [Khomeini] came down the steps from the plane in Iran where he changed…The mullahs got a hold of him and gave him a new destiny, which is the dictatorship we see today."[76]

Bani-Sadr was fortunate enough to leave Iran and live another forty years in France. Under Ayatollah Khomeini, Iranians, particularly women and minorities, were stripped of many civil and political liberties. Many of Khomeini's other partners in the broadly popular anti-shah movement quickly suffered much worse fates. As Khomeini maneuvered from an Iranian Revolution to an Islamic Revolution with him as the unquestioned leader, his regime executed hundreds of leftists, communists, Kurds, and others who had gravely misjudged Khomeini.

Rather than deciding to represent a nation, Khomeini's nascent Islamic Republic opted to represent a fundamentalist cause, one that isolated the country further from the international community and which coerced its civilian population into acquiescence.[77] However, Iranians' acceptance of the brutal rule of the Islamic Republic's security state has never been absolute.

Three Movements: 2009, 2017, 2019

The Mahsa Amini protests set off in late 2022 were scarcely the first major explosion of civil unrest in the history of modern Iran, or even of the Islamic Republic. While the regime has grown adept at brutally stamping out protest movements once they emerge, it has been less successful at preventing their recurrence. A culture of protest and dissent has, in fact, existed for much of the theocracy's forty-six years in power.

Thirty years after the Islamic Revolution of 1979 and 100 years after the Constitutional Revolution of 1906-11, a tremendous spirit of change swept Iran. Forty million voters headed to the voting booths for the presidential elections on June 12, 2009. For weeks, there had been a growing wave of support for reformist hopeful Mir Hossein Mousavi, the leading opposition candidate to the incumbent Mahmoud Ahmadinejad. Reliable figures suggested that at least 80-85 percent of eligible voters in Iran showed up to the voting booths, emboldened by the prospect of real change taking place within the existing system of government.

Mousavi's manifesto—de-prioritizing nuclear proliferation, advancing economic and social reforms, and encouraging greater interaction with the

Western world—was diametrically opposed to Ahmadinejad's, whose platform doubled down on an anti-Western, isolationist and socially conservative approach that rejected nuclear negotiations and favored conflict with the United States and Israel. Still, against this backdrop, and a year after Barack Obama was elected President of the United States over John McCain, Mousavi appeared to have cultivated a groundswell of support among the Iranian electorate who sought a different approach for Iran. As one journalist covering the 2009 presidential elections put it:[78]

"The run-up to the elections was unlike anything that the generations that grew up after the 1979 revolution had ever experienced. On these nights the police left the campaigners alone. It was as if a breeze of liberty was blowing through the streets. The cries and slogans that resounded were voicing demands which did not conflict with the Constitution...

For the first time in the Islamic Republic's election history, candidates debated with each other in the American style; publicly before the people. Heated words were exchanged about the country's current policies on a platform provided by the media whose head is selected by the Leader...The televised debates caused an immediate reaction. The slumber that had characterized these years was left behind and people exploded out into the streets. The enthusiasm over the elections was at its peak."

The 2009 elections saw a record turnout. Mousavi was widely expected to beat, or at least significantly challenge, Ahmadinejad if there had been a high turnout. But elections in Iran are seldom free or fair. One way the regime has been able to cement its longevity is by purging reformists, stripping them of any influence and confining real power to the inner core of Khomeinists and Khameneists. The atmosphere soured shortly after polling closed when Ahmadinejad went on to record a crushing victory, clinching 63 percent of the vote.

The 2009 Green Movement that emerged following the results of the election rejected hard-liner Mahmoud Ahmadinejad's victory over Mousavi.[79] Protesters claimed the election was rigged in favor of Ahmadinejad, stamping out hopes of increased social freedoms in Iran and greater integration with the West. Soon, cries of "Where Is My Vote?" reverberated across Iran, becoming the rally cry of the Green Movement.

Mousavi himself rejected the results of the election, declaring himself the real winner and issuing a warning directly to Ayatollah Khamenei. "I personally strongly protest the many dangerous obvious violations and I'm warning I will not surrender to this dangerous charade," said Mousavi, adding, "the result will jeopardize the pillars of the Islamic Republic and establish tyranny."[80] Khamenei dismissed Mousavi's claims and urged him and the other losing opposition candidates to support the outcome of the election and avoid "provocative" behavior, adding that, "All Iranians must support and help the elected president."

On June 15, 2009, as many as three million people gathered in Tehran to protest what they saw as a gross form of political corruption and electoral fraud.[81] "How is it possible that Mousavi didn't even get good results in his own province?" said Samaneh Younes, a bewildered nurse demonstrating in Tehran's Vanak Square. "How is it possible that there were no blank votes? Why didn't the government provide enough ballots in big cities where Mousavi had a huge number of supporters?"[82]

As with the Mahsa Amini protests of 2022, Tehran's leadership in 2009 was sitting on an explosive powder keg of social discontent and economic misery waiting to be ignited. Millions lined the streets of Iran's major cities, condemning political oppression and calling for an annulment of the electoral outcome. At the time, the Green Movement represented the most serious threat to the theocratic establishment since 1979.

In the Middle East and North Africa, big events oftentimes have small, unexpected beginnings. Around the time of the Green Movement in Iran, other countries in the region began experiencing a surge of their own pro-democracy protests and uprisings. In Tunisia, a "Jasmine Revolution" was set off after twenty-six-year-old fruit and vegetable street vendor Mohamed Bouazizi set himself on fire in the town of Sidi Bouzid to protest against the local government's corruption and brutality. Bouazizi's self-immolation sparked revolutions across the region. Waves of pro-democracy unrest in Tunisia and Egypt led to government overthrows and absolute regime change, triggering an "Arab Spring" in the rest of the Arab world, with

Bahrain, Libya, Syria and Yemen also staging popular uprisings of their own against ruling regimes, albeit with less success.

So too in Iran, people were zealous for reform, although demonstrators' rage was met with violent government repression. Hundreds were beaten and arrested. Dozens were killed by the Islamic Revolutionary Guard Corps. And, like the "Woman, Life, Freedom" protests, the 2009 Green Movement also had female martyr figures.

Among them was twenty-six-year-old Neda Agha-Soltan, whose grim death mirrored Mahsa Jina Amini's thirteen years later. Like many Iranians her age, elements of Agha-Soltan's life seemed surprisingly Western to outsiders. She divorced at a young age and loved to sing and play the violin, hanging a poster of Dire Straits guitarist Mark Knopfler on her bedroom wall.[83] While learning Turkish to work as tour guide for Iranians in Turkey, she met a new fiancé. She was a philosophy major and interested in underground music. She was in many ways an ordinary woman navigating life in Iran as best she could.

However, the end of her life reflected the reality of the Iranian police state. Like Amini, Agha-Soltan was killed not because of any particularly notable activism, but because of the violence visited upon civilians who have made the mistake of being in the vicinity of an opposition protest. On June 20, 2009, Agha-Soltan got stuck in traffic near a protest; a friend of hers later said she wasn't even a supporter of Mousavi. She exited her car and, shortly afterwards, was shot in the chest by a member of the Basij paramilitary forces. The shooter was grabbed by the crowd and identified before being released, but he was never prosecuted. A doctor next to Agha-Soltan who unsuccessfully tried to save her life later fled the country after confirming to media that a Basij member had killed her.[84] Agha-Soltan's relatives were not allowed to publicly mourn her death.[85]

Agha-Soltan's gruesome, bloody death was filmed on grainy cell phone footage and disseminated by opposition websites and media outlets, fanning outrage and turning her into a powerful symbol of opposition to the Islamic Republic. At the time, it was described as the "most watched death in human history."[86] One opposition candidate who ran in the 2009 presidential elections, Mehdi Karroubi, called Agha-Soltan a martyr, adding: "A young girl, who did not have a weapon in her soft hands, or a grenade in her pocket, became a victim of thugs who are supported by a horrifying intelligence apparatus."[87]

However, the death of this innocent young woman failed to create the same momentum as Amini's murder. There are many possible explanations for this difference. For one, social media was more prevalent in 2022 and Agha-Soltan wasn't killed specifically over the repressive hijab laws. The single most likely explanation is that the 2009 protests took place in a different political context. In 2009, people stormed the streets in the name of reform, demanding that their votes be properly counted. Agha-Soltan's death caused shock, but there was a bigger cause. By 2022, hopes for reform were nearly dead. Protesters were not reform-oriented. They wanted to tear down the whole edifice. Amini's death was a spark for intense, frustrated rage.

Protests in Iran continued well into 2010, but the agitation eventually subsided after the reformist movement's leadership was excommunicated and put under house arrest. Mir Hossein Mousavi, who previously served as Prime Minister and was a leading opposition figure in the 2009 presidential elections, remains under house arrest. Today, political parties endorsing sweeping changes and reforms are largely banned or marginalized from Iranian politics.

For some, the Green Movement wasn't an abject failure and had an indelible effect on Iranian society still felt today. "If we consider Iran's pro-democracy "Green Movement" not as a revolution but as a civil rights movement—as the leaders of the movement do—then a "win" must be measured over time," wrote Iranian journalist Hooman Majd in *Foreign Policy* in 2010.[88] "It's evident that the Green Movement has already "won" in many respects, if a win means that many Iranians are no longer resigned to the undemocratic aspects of a political system that has in the last three decades regressed, rather than progressed, in affording its citizens the rights promised to them under Iran's own Constitution."

In 2017, a storm of labor protests erupted over the price of eggs and broader economic dislocations. The protests recurred in 2018 in response to exorbitant gas prices, and quickly spread to seventy-five cities across Iran.

In 2019, fuel prices skyrocketed overnight in a 50-to-200 percent increase, spurring more protests. Those bursts of unrest were led predominantly by low-income young men, who were most negatively impacted by unaffordable food and gas prices. As with past periods of unrest in Iran, the protests soon turned into larger expressions of popular discontent over the government's repression, mismanagement of the economy and flagrant corruption.

Woman, Life, Freedom Protests, 2022-2023

Well before 2022, modern Iranian history was replete with protest movements that started locally and gained traction, rapidly morphing into major catalysts for political change. These popular opposition movements can be broadly divided into two categories. The first, less threatening, and most common type of insurrection is limited in scope and concerns a localized issue, whether that be spiraling food and gas prices, high unemployment, or low wages.

Most of the movements in Iran's recent history have been led by Iranian individuals and groups demanding changes within the framework of the Islamic Republic's system of government. Whether those calls were heeded or not, these types of revolt seldom challenged the regime in ways that were existential. I term these fleeting bouts of protest: "ephemeral, issue-based revolts." The Green Movement in 2009 that erupted over a disputed presidential election rigged in favor of government favorite Mahmoud Ahmadinejad, is a pertinent example of an issue-based revolt. The protests gained considerable momentum and global attention, but the protesters were ultimately pushing for reforms within the current framework of government in Iran.

The "Woman, Life, Freedom" protesters were entirely different. They were not seeking reformist change from within. Endless state repression, corruption and economic mismanagement had pushed them over the edge. They were done with Ayatollah Khamenei, the Islamic Republic and the entire totalitarian system of government. They clamored to upend the theocratic regime's foundations through substantive regime change. I call these revolutions "existential revolts."

The sheer durability of the latest wave of protests in 2022 and 2023 was also notable when considering the relative ease with which the Iranian government stamped out past outbursts of revolt in 2009, 2017, and 2019.

Another dramatic difference with the protests that started in 2022 was that, for the first time in Iran's history, women became both the symbols and driving force of a revolutionary movement. But their calls for change also transcended women's rights, encompassing freedom and enfranchisement, a call to action against tyranny and political repression against a theocratic institution that since its inception in 1979 had unreservedly targeted women's freedom.[89]

"This corrupt regime will do anything to stay where they are," a female protester told the *BBC* in early December 2022. "We the protesters don't care about 'no hijab' [anymore]…We've been going out without it for the past seventy days. A revolution is what we care [about]—hijab was the start of it, and we don't want anything less than death for the dictator [Ali Khamenei], and regime change."[90]

The Mahsa Amini protests were unprecedented, exposing deep societal and political fissures that continue to pose a profound and enduring threat to the regime's stability.

Resilience of Revolt

While the street protests that exploded in September of 2022 had largely subsided by mid-2023, the legacy of civil disobedience has persisted. Strict modesty rules for women remain in place in Iran, but more women than ever are walking in public with their hair unveiled, in large part because of the Mahsa Amini protest movement. One Iranian visitor to the United Kingdom in 2024 had even noted that there were more veils visible on London's underground than in Tehran's metro.[91] This personal defiance continues, despite being met with extreme violence.

On July 21, 2024, Nafas Haji Sharif and her friend, both fourteen-years-old, had planned a shopping trip on Vatanpour Street in northern Tehran.

On their way, multiple female morality police officers stationed in Tehran violently attacked them for having their hair uncovered. They were both forced into a van, where they were brutally beaten. Haji Sharif, who was left with deep scars and bruises on her neck and face, later said of the ordeal: "They [morality police] were pulling me by my hair, shouting at me and cursing…when they took me inside the van, they threw me onto the floor. One female agent hit me, put her knee on my throat, and hit my head hard. My head was stuck between the seats, and they were kicking the side of my torso."[92]

A day later, on July 22, 2024, thirty-one-year-old Arezou Badri, a mother of two driving home with her sister in the northern city of Noor, was shot in her car by authorities over an alleged violation of the country's mandatory hijab laws. One bullet was aimed at the car's tire. The second bullet was aimed at the driver's seat, penetrating Badri's lung and severely, possibly irreversibly, damaging her spinal cord.[93]

Forty-six years into its rule, the Islamic Republic has been unforgiving in brutally squashing protest movements. Its instinct to sense, and destroy, revolutionary fervor among disgruntled Iranian citizens can be explained in part because it too came about as a result of a revolution, ousting the Shah and extinguishing the Pahlavi dynasty in 1979. Not only did the nascent theocratic leadership know what it took to execute a successful revolution, but it has since known how to violently and resoundingly stamp out burgeoning uprisings or sparks of unrest that might eventually avalanche into a revolution.

Khomeini's words in the early days of his revolution hint at why the Mahsa Amini protests are particularly sensitive to the system he helped establish: "Every time a female body brushes up against a male body on a bus, a tremor shakes the edifice of our revolution." In other words, women were uniquely threatening to the Islamic Republic. For forty-six years, the Islamic Republic has tied itself to the relegated status of women and the enforcement of the hijab. In this sort of oppositional stance, neither the government nor protesters can see room for reform.

CHAPTER 5
SOCIAL MEDIA IN IRAN

"We are in need of joy and recreation. Good spirits, good vibes, good energy. In order to have these, we need freedom."
—Sarina Esmailzadeh, sixteen-year-old student and vlogger, 2022

On February 17, 2023, Zeinab Kazempour walked onstage at an annual assembly of Iran's professional association of engineers in Tehran with two messages. The first was delivered by way of her appearance: underneath an imposing image of the Supreme Leader, Ayatollah Ali Khamenei, Kazempour appeared with her long brown hair uncovered and tied in a ponytail, in violation of the country's strict hijab laws.

Her second message was verbal. After being banned from running for the association's board of directors, she introduced herself and said: "I don't recognize the assembly that doesn't allow candidates to run because they don't wear a headscarf."[94] She then exited the stage to rapturous applause and symbolically tossed her scarf next to the image of Khamenei. Then, her brief moment of dissent was amplified many times over as it went viral on social media.

The 1979 Islamic Revolution was among the most televised revolts in history. Images of throngs of people in the streets of Tehran were beamed around the world. Today, mass protests and demonstrations in Iran take place in a dramatically different media environment. Every act of indefatigable courage—or public instance of outrageous government repression—is not only documented, but shared widely in nearly real time, inspiring new acts of courage and protest.

One such example came in the northeastern city of Shandiz in April 2023. CCTV footage from a modestly-sized grocery store showed a man in a red checkered shirt angrily confront two women with their heads uncovered before grabbing tubs of yogurt from the refrigerator and dumping them on the women's heads. The male shop owner, shocked, forcefully threw out the man. However, the two women were the ones who ended up being arrested for failing to wear the compulsory hijab in public, sparking outrage.

Force Multiplier

The widespread use of social media in Iran long predates the Mahsa Amini protests. Starting with the 2009 Green Revolution, the impact of organizing and information sharing via the internet, specifically social media apps, has had a profound impact on the nature and scope of protests in Iran, and the rest of the world. And social media's reach is greater than it was in 2009. A 2021 survey carried out by the government-run Iranian Students Polling Agency (ISPA) found that 73 percent of Iranians over eighteen used social media and messaging applications.[95] This means that when the posts on Twitter and WhatsApp detailing Mahsa Amini's mistreatment and death first appeared, roughly three out of four Iranians had direct access to them. A massive nationwide wave of protest was more likely to occur when so many people could see repression and protests unfolding on their phones. And, as the anti-government demonstrations continued, social media posts about state violence in one region of Iran quickly spread via a web of social media apps to the rest of the country, providing more fuel for protesters' anger.

The story of nine-year-old Kian Pirfalak sparked such outrage. Before becoming a symbol of the regime's brutality—and likely the youngest victim of the government's bloody crackdown on protesters—Pirfalak dreamed of becoming a robotics engineer and inventor. That all ended on November 16, 2022, when Pirfalak's parents and younger brother were driving through protests in Izeh, a small, primarily Bakhtiari, city in southwestern Iran. The protests were fervent, with clips on social media showing demonstrators chanting "This is the year of blood, Seyed Ali [Khamenei] will be overthrown."[96]

Suddenly, plainclothes officers started spraying bullets at Pirfalak's car. Zeinab Molairad, Kian's mother, recalled telling her kids to rush to the ground of the car underneath the seat as soon as the shooting started. "My little one was underneath the dashboard. I don't know why [Kian] didn't go. He was chubby. He didn't go under the seat," she said.[97]

A grainy social media video soon after the ordeal showed a man and woman crying helplessly beside Pirfalak's lifeless body, shouting, "This is the result of the Islamic Republic! This is the result of the Islamic Republic!"

The family came under severe pressure from the government to refrain from speaking out about the circumstances of Kian's death, but they resisted. "We declare that we witnessed the killing of our child and the injuring of Meysam Pirfalak (the father) by the shooting of judiciary agents on our private vehicle and we have filed a complaint against them,"[98] read a statement issued by the Pirfalak family and then published on social media. Zeinab Molairad, the boy's mother, subsequently lost her job as a teacher for displaying such insubordination.

Iran's security forces denied being involved in Pirfalak's death, claiming that the boy was killed by errant bullets fired by terrorists unconnected to the government. Then, about a month after the shooting, on December 20, 2022, police detained a street protester named Mojahed Kourkour and, following a kangaroo trial, found him guilty of killing Kian Pirfalak and sentenced him to death, even as the Pirfalak family maintained Kourkour's innocence. The Iranian government wielded immense power in detaining and executing protesters, but it could do nothing to stop the shocking image of Kian Pirfalak's dead body—and the belief that government forces killed him—from beaming around the country and world.

With much of the nationwide uprising playing out on the internet, forcefully quelling widespread street protests was no longer enough for Iran's security forces. Within days of Amini's death in September 2022, social media was replete with anti-government hashtags, anti-Khamenist slogans and videos and a flood of clips showing Iranians openly defying the Islamic Republic and its strict hijab laws. Videos spread online of women, including female high school and college students, defiantly waving their head scarves in the air while chanting *zan, zendegi, azadi* ("Woman, Life, Freedom") and shouting *marg bar dictator* ("Death to the Dictator!")

Fueling the Fire

Even if social media was unsuccessful at checking state violence toward protesters, it did at least create consequences in the form of a vivid and immediate feedback loop. Rather than discouraging protests in one area, the widely shared images of brutal crackdowns by the government simply intensified the anger already directed at the Islamic Republic.

In November 2022, Mohsen Shekari—a young barista who lived in Tehran—was arbitrarily accused of blocking a main road in Tehran and attacking a member of the Islamic Republic's security forces with a machete. Shekari's family was only informed that he would be put to death after he was hanged. Following his execution, Shekari was hurriedly buried in *Behesht-e Zahra*—a sprawling cemetery, the largest in Iran, with over a million graves located to the south of Tehran—with only a few family members permitted to attend the funeral.

If the secretive haste was meant to cover up Shekari's killing, it failed. Footage from the day of Shekari's execution showed a female relative of his bellowing out in the streets "Oh, Mohsen" as she learned of Shekari's fate. The night following Shekari's burial, a viral video showed a long vertical poster being unfurled on a Tehran highway with a woman talking over the video saying: "Dear Mohsen, you only closed one street, but very soon we will close all of Iran." Other social media videos showed Iranians across the country shouting, "Death to Khamenei, the murderer."

Shekari's death marked the first execution of a protester convicted since the "Woman, Life, Freedom" protests first broke out. He would not be the last. By the summer of 2023, seven more Iranians were executed by regime forces, with more sitting on death row. Because of social media coverage, their plights were not a secret, but rapidly fueled more outrage and drove more protesters onto the streets.

During the 2022-2023 protests, the Islamic Republic had to contend with the fact that, though its large security apparatus was able to control many aspects of Iranians' lives, managing social media and the internet more broadly was a far greater endeavor. At the start of the "Woman, Life, Freedom" protests, the government cut off internet access in parts of Kurdistan and Tehran, according to NetBlocks, a watchdog agency monitoring internet freedom worldwide, and shut down WhatsApp and Instagram for fear of more Iranians finding out about the rapid spread of social unrest across the country.[99] The regime also had the capacity to censor and limit information flow through the Telecommunication Infrastructure Company of Iran, which is controlled by Iran's security and surveillance apparatus.

In response to ongoing government attempts to shut down social media, millions of Iranians relied on virtual private networks (VPNs) to conceal their internet activity from state censors even before 2022. VPNs work by encrypting users' data and masking their IP addresses, making it more difficult to track and identify a user's location.

The Iranian government was so concerned about its struggle to control the proliferation of VPNs that Ruhollah Momen Nasab, an Iranian official responsible for internet affairs and digital media, declared that those found to be selling VPNs should be executed for "corruption of the earth."[100] The massive surge in censorship as the protests continued—and the subsequently accelerated shift to VPN-encrypted usage—explains why Iran had the sharpest drop in internet access globally in 2023, according to Freedom House, a Washington, D.C. nonprofit focused on democracy and political freedom.[101]

In addition to VPNs, protesters also switched to Telegram, Instagram, and other social media platforms to disseminate information that circumvented the regime's internet censors. An anonymous Iranian immigrant in Los Angeles also helped out protesters through their group NetFreedom Pioneers, which devised a way to broadcast text, audio and video files via satellite dishes, allowing information to bypass the internet entirely. NetFreedom Pioneers collected information about the protests, including photos and social media news, and beamed them into homes in Iran with receiver dishes. The news was spread further offline via USB flash drives.[102] Lasting change in Iran will likely only come from within, but the ability of social media to get information into, out of and around the country served as a potent weapon against regime misinformation and repression.

Revolution Gone Virtual

The "Woman, Life, Freedom" protests were a dramatic demonstration of social media making the world more interconnected than ever before.

Young Iranian men and women are just like young people elsewhere in the world. They have dreams and goals, both professional and personal, are boundlessly creative, and worry about their future. While the Islamic Republic has succeeded in controlling most aspects of social and cultural life in Iran, social media and the internet have offered Iranians greater access to the outside world, where they can interact with contemporaries and imagine, or even actualize, a different future for themselves.

Likewise, young people outside of Iran can better appreciate ordinary Iranians beyond the stereotypes and clickbait headlines, while separating the country's repressive government from its extraordinary society and rich culture. The internet and social media have for years served as windows for Iranians into the outside world, a digital portal teasing them with the promise of what could be.

As such, the internet creates a unique problem for any authoritarian regime. To be economically viable, every country needs its young people to be technically savvy, which means making sure they have access to computers and the internet. However, doing so means losing absolute control over the information flowing into, and out of, the country. The globality of social media means that young Iranians have grown up with one foot in a world where people have freedoms and lifestyles unimaginable in their home country. People Amini's age have grown up exposed to an entirely different set of values than those of the Islamic Republic.

During my interview with Reza Pahlavi, the exiled Crown Prince of Iran and a frequent commentator on social and political events in his country, he explained that social media had played a role in undermining one of the core tenets of the Islamic Revolution: that the U.S., or Great Satan, is the greatest enemy of Iran. "If you follow Iranian social media, you will see to what extent Iranians are, in fact, enamored by, and focused on, the promise of freedom that the West offers. If you were to open the embassies in Tehran tomorrow, there'll be a mile long line for people to get a visa to come to the United States. That's how the people in Iran perceive the outside world, particularly America, as opposed to the regime."[103]

As a result of social media, Iran's youth, like other young people worldwide, are more focused on body positivity, fashion, consumerism, and self-image than older generations. That, in part, explains the revolutionary fervor displayed by Iran's younger generation and their refusal to abide by the regime's anachronistic hijab laws, a phenomenon termed by Iranian journalist and activist Noushin Ahmadi Khorasani in 2018 as the "selfie" phenomenon.[104] Social media has changed the way Iran's youth imagine themselves in a way that is fundamentally incongruous to the way of life set out by the Islamic Republic. "For today's generation of girls," Khorasani wrote in *Radio Zamaneh*, a Persian-language news outlet based in the Netherlands, "the objection to the compulsory hijab...has turned into an assault and attack on their individual identity."

Double Life

Among the young Iranians who grew up exposed to social media was Sarina Esmailzadeh, a sixteen-year-old avid YouTube vlogger, who diarized her daily life as a Gen-Zer in Iran. In her vlogs, she would chronicle the limitations imposed on her as a female born in Iran compared to the more independent lives of her contemporaries who she followed in Los Angeles and New York.

"Good God, let me give you my life, take me to church," she sang during a family road trip to Kashan, in central Iran, mimicking artist Hozier's 2013 hit song. This was her first YouTube video, titled "My First Vlog!" The video was replete with cultural references to Western music and popular TV shows like "Breaking Bad" and "SpongeBob SquarePants."

Esmailzadeh spoke about the profound and mundane aspects of life in Iran, from how she likes to put on makeup and make pizza meals for her family, to her struggles conforming to the country's strict hijab laws, the future of the country, the key role of education in creating a better, more prosperous Iran, and how some of her favorite historic sites in the country had been mismanaged or destroyed by the government.

Esmailzadeh's videos were not just a pastime of hers. Aware of the consequences of speaking out, she used her burgeoning YouTube platform—with more than 20,000 subscribers and 1.8 million total views on her videos—to challenge some of the most deep-rooted conventions in the Islamic Republic, whether it be appearing without a headscarf, singing in public, praising Western culture, disagreeing with conventional wisdom or socializing freely with people of the opposite gender.

"We all know what state Iran is in today," Esmailzadeh lamented in one of her vlogs called "Iranian youth fight!" published on May 22, 2022, racking up 118,000 views. She added, "What can people expect from their own country? Prosperity! But our economic conditions are terrible, our cultural conditions are terrible and our authenticity is being destroyed. Limitations are especially tough on women, like the mandatory hijab…I have always asked myself: why? Why should my life be so different [to the lives of teenagers elsewhere in the Western world]? Just because I was born in Iran?" In her final YouTube vlog, published on July 12, 2022, Esmailzadeh signed off with: "If I don't see you…bye!"

On September 23, Iranian security forces in Karaj beat Esmailzadeh to death with baton strikes to the head. Iranian authorities rejected claims that Esmailzadeh had died at the hands of the Islamic Republic's security forces, accusing Esmailzadeh of having been immoral and engaging in terrorist activities, eventually concluding that she had been suicidal, jumping off a multi-story building to her death. Esmailzadeh's badly beaten body was not handed back to her family for over a week. Local news outlets had reported that Esmailzadeh's family had been harassed by security forces in an attempt to silence them. When authorities finally returned Esmailzadeh to her family, her body was battered beyond recognition. Security forces continued to taunt Esmailzadeh's family until her mother, unable to cope with the murder of her daughter, hanged herself.[105]

Once again, the social media feedback loop between protesters and state oppression kicked in: News of Esmailzadeh's death quickly spread through Iran, prompting high schoolers all over the country to take a stand, staging mass protests of their own. Despite intense internet blackouts, social media footage showed teenage students, and in some cases teachers, ripping off their hijabs and singing anti-government chants in open defiance of a regime that had claimed the lives of Sarina and so many more young women who wanted to live in an Iran that was free and fair for people of all regardless of gender, ethnicity, or religion. Concealing their faces and with their hair flowing freely, they brandished posters of Mahsa Amini and other brave women, chanted "Woman, Life, Freedom" and shouted obscenities at the clerical establishment.

High schoolers across Iran continued to stage anti-government protests, even as thousands of schoolgirls were struck down by chemical poisoning attacks. Human rights groups reported that between November 2022 and March 2023, some 7,000 schoolgirls were poisoned across dozens of schools in at least twenty-eight of Iran's thirty-one provinces.[106] Some suspected the government of orchestrating these attacks as retribution for the schoolgirls' hijab violations and for joining in the protests. The regime denied any wrongdoing. In March 2023, Khamenei denied any government involvement in the chemical attacks, describing the poisonings as an "unforgivable" crime that should be punishable with the death penalty.[107]

Hozier, whose hit song "Take Me to Church" Esmailzadeh belted out in her popular vlog, spoke out about the protests in Iran after learning of the sixteen-year-old's horrific death. The Iranian regime could brutalize its own people, but could do little to control the Irish singer-songwriter's viral rebuke. "The story of Sarina Esmailzadeh reached me this morning," Hozier told his one million followers on X on October 7, 2022. "I'm somewhat at a loss for words. We talk about freedoms with no understanding of what it means to pay the ultimate price in fighting for it."[108]

"Tehrangeles"

Mahsa Amini's story resonated with so many Iranians both inside Iran and abroad because it could have been them, accosted in the streets, arrested and beaten to death by a regime that places little value on life. Hundreds of women had already been harassed by the country's security forces before Amini, and no doubt there have been more since. Such repression drove many Iranians to flee the country in recent decades, with an estimated four million Iranians scattered across the diaspora today.

Many Iranians in the diaspora today romanticize about the Iran they, their parents and grandparents once knew, but can't return to while the current theocracy remains in power. Older Iranians living in America today mostly left their homeland around the time of the 1979 Islamic Revolution.

Many of those Iranians who left Iran for the United States in the late 1970s settled in Los Angeles, known affectionately as "Tehrangeles" for having a similar climate to Tehran and being home to the world's largest Iranian community outside of Iran itself. More than half a million Iranians and Iranian-Americans live in America today, with approximately 40 percent settling in California.

The other side of social media's global reach has been the connection, or re-connection, of people abroad with ordinary Iranians. The four-million-person Iranian diaspora had previously relied on influential Persian language TV channels including *Iran International*, *BBC Persian* and *Manoto TV* to stay apprised of events inside their home country. Social media gave them a much more direct and unvarnished window into daily life inside the country.

Just as social media amplified the news of Amini's arrest and subsequent death within Iran, it also galvanized external support for the protesters and pressure on the government. Early on in the Mahsa Amini protests, ordinary Iranians realized that social media was the only tool at their disposal to ensure their voices would be heard by the world. And it was Western governments and citizens seeing young, bold Iranians fighting for the same needs and wants of young people everywhere that stirred the international community to stand with the people of Iran.

For years, Iranian netizens have harnessed the creative tools of social media and messaging platforms to satirize, censure, vent and organize. Especially since access to Iran is severely limited for independent and foreign journalists, Iranian netizens and citizen journalists have played an outsized role in documenting past protests and the trajectory of the Mahsa Amini uprising—all while fighting for the dignity and equal treatment of Iranian women and girls.

Since the start of the protests, young Iranians have been filming the unrest and government violence themselves and posting it online for the world to see. *PBS Frontline's* "Inside the Iranian Uprising," released in the summer of 2023, was a moving documentary chronicling the sheer bravery of the young Iranians who took part in the "Woman, Life, Freedom" protests. Much of the footage shown in the documentary was drawn from more than 100 hours of video shot mostly by young Iranians on their mobile phones. By Iranians who wanted the outside world to see what the state had tried to suppress.

Actual cell phone footage of the "Woman, Life, Freedom" protests was also incorporated into *The Seed of the Sacred Fig*, a groundbreaking Oscar-nominated movie released in late November 2024. Created by Iranian director Mohammad Rasoulof, the film was shot inside Iran in secret, with Rasoulof fleeing the country on foot after being sentenced to eight years in prison. The film centers on a nuclear family in Tehran. Iman, the father, is an investigator for the regime's Revolutionary Court tasked with rubber-stamping the execution of young protesters. As the protests surge in Tehran, Iman's teenage daughters, Rezvan and Sana, grow increasingly sympathetic to the protests unfolding in real time via social media on their phones, something that was actively being ignored or dismissed on state TV.

Tech's Dark Side

For all the advantages social media and internet connectivity provide to people opposing an authoritarian state, technology has also been used to intensify the clerical regime's Orwellian grip over its people who express dissent on the streets and in cyberspace. On the ground, the Islamic

Republic controls its population through mass arrests and physical crackdowns. Online, it imposes restrictive internet filtering systems to silence loud opponents, while deploying cyber agents—known as *Cyberi*—to hack and spear-phish dissidents, journalists, scholars and policy experts abroad. Spear-phishing refers to precise, well-researched cyber attacks typically focused on high-profile targets—like a spoof email address of a CEO messaging finance executives in their company to carry out financial transactions—usually in the hope of extracting money or sensitive information, or infecting the targets' device with malware.[109]

While digital technologies are these days essential to the decentralized organizing of demonstrations, the Islamic Republic has often turned it against activists. In February 2023, for example, the popular anti-regime social media account "RKOT" (Rich Kids of Tehran), with half a million followers combined on Instagram and X, revealed that it had received an interview request from someone purporting to be a *New York Times* journalist. During their attempt to verify the request, the group eventually traced the original IP address of the sender not to a *Times* bureau, but to an IRGC intelligence headquarters located in Shiraz, in southwestern Iran. "The email," RKOT said in a later tweet, "was a fake. A warning to everyone!"[110]

Aware of the heightened vigilance about hacking attempts, IRGC cyber agents have become creative in their approach. One method the agency has employed includes setting up fake social media accounts that build up credibility by conspicuously criticizing the Islamic Republic and amplifying the voices of the opposition in order to gain credibility. "Sara Shokouhi" was one such example.[111] Created in October 2022, her Twitter profile claimed she had completed a PhD in Middle Eastern Politics from Northwestern State University of Louisiana and was employed at the Atlantic Council, a Washington, D.C.-based think tank. An image of a Russian psychologist posing by a stack of books completed the profile. Retweeting opposition voices and tributes to the "Woman, Life, Freedom" protesters, Shokouhi's account hardly aroused suspicion. But eventually the account was outed as a persona concocted by regime-linked hackers who were part of the Iranian

"Cobalt Illusion" threat group and had been targeting a number of Iran-focused researchers through phishing and email compromise campaigns.[112]

Longtime activist Majid Tavakoli, currently serving a sentence in Evin Prison, has argued that the digital and internet technology often seen as liberating and essential to the leaderless organizing of demonstrations simultaneously makes it harder to organize within the country. "Unfortunately," said Tavakoli, "technology has also contributed to repression…The government can now do far more with telecommunications monitoring and surveillance cameras. It can impose financial penalties [like] closing bank accounts and other transactions. The manipulation of truth and consciousness has also changed. In other words, this technology has led us to face more control and propaganda instead of suppression and censorship."[113]

Nika's Nightmare

Leading up to Amini's death, in late June 2022 a group of teenagers gathered in the city of Shiraz for a skating event.[114] Videos shot in the park that day showed some of the girls were not wearing a hijab as they mingled. Following the casual gathering, at least ten of the young participants on the video were arrested, and the event was lambasted by local authorities for ushering in "the age of nudity."

During the "Woman, Life, Freedom" protests, the dangers of appearing on social media still existed, but as the protests intensified, the government's reaction to dissent online became more violent. Like Sarina Esmailzadeh, Nika Shakarami was sixteen and an avid social media user who participated in non-violent protests against the regime in late 2022. For them, social media was not just a tool to document the brutal reality of everyday life under the Islamic Republic, but also highlighted their generation's social need to connect, at least in cyberspace when real-life interactions were being closely regulated and stymied. Unfortunately, their use of social media also made them targets for state repression.

On September 20, 2022, at approximately 7:10 p.m. local time, Shakarami, who studied in art high school and worked in a cafe, was seen participating in another protest by Laleh Park in central Tehran. Videos online showed Shakarami, clad in black and wearing a mask, standing on top of a large garbage container that had been tipped over, while waving her hijab that was set on fire and chanting with the crowd, "Death to the dictator." Shakarami, who was an ethnic Lur, had also thrown rocks at the anti-riot police who responded forcefully by firing tear gas and pellets at protesters. Shortly afterwards, Shakarami vanished. Her Instagram and Telegram accounts were deleted. She was unreachable, with her phone switched off.

Shakarami's mother, Nasrin, had no idea where her daughter was, so she plastered photos of her on social media in the hope that someone had seen her. "We went to the prisons, the police and to many other places—we went everywhere we could think of," Nasrin recalled. Finally, on September 29, nine days later, Nasrin found her daughter's lifeless body in the morgue of the Kahrizak detention center.

Eyewitness accounts and social media footage appeared to suggest that Shakarami had been tracked down by Iranian security authorities the night of September 20, with one key witness recalling that she saw Shakarami forcibly taken into custody by "several large-bodied plainclothes security offices" who threw her into a car and likely beat her to death shortly thereafter.[115] Disturbing reports by the *BBC* even found that the undercover agents who had detained Shakarami—members of a unit in Iran's security apparatus known as Team 12—had sexually assaulted her while she was bound and gagged in a nondescript freezer van.

When inspecting her daughter's body in the morgue, Nasrin observed that "her hands, her feet and her body were undamaged, but her face and cheek bones were broken, her teeth were knocked out and the back of her head had been hit so hard it caved in."

Iranian authorities vehemently denied these claims, asserting that Shakarami had died at a later point in time in an uninhabited building under circumstances that had nothing to do with the anti-government protests. Mohammad Shahriari, who headed the criminal prosecution division in Tehran province, stated that Shakarami died after entering an unknown building hours after the protests and had either jumped off the roof of the building in an act of suicide, or had been pushed by a non-government assailant. Shahriari cited as evidence an autopsy that showed fractures all over Shakarami's body, from her head, upper and lower limbs, pelvis, hip, hands and feet, adding that "an investigation showed this incident had no connection to the protests. No bullet holes were found on the body."[116]

Shakarami's mother, Nasrin, remained unconvinced by the state's findings, claiming in an Instagram post that residents living close to where Shakarami's body was found said they saw a group of men drop off a dead girl's body to the scene while spraying a red substance that resembled blood in what appeared to be a staged death.[117]

Shakarami's funeral on October 2, 2022—also her seventeenth birthday—was a somber affair, with her aunt inviting the public to attend on social media. "You are invited to attend Nika's last birthday," she wrote. "Nika, who is no longer with us, will always be here. May the death of our brave Nika give rise to millions and millions of other Nikas."[118]

Days after Shakarami's death, her aunt and uncle were arrested. Shakarami's aunt was forced to sign a forced confession confirming that her niece had indeed fallen off a building to her death.

"I don't accept these stories," Shakarami's mother told *PBS Frontline*. "The Islamic Republic and the Revolutionary Guard Corps killed Nika...They are not taking responsibility for killing her, nor are they telling us who did. They are not pursuing the case. I am a mother and I loved Nika infinitely."[119]

To a regime anathema to change, Shakarami, like scores of other young brave girls, represented a grave threat. As such, the regime silenced her by taking her life away and by expunging her social media profiles. Since then, at least one major tech company, Meta, has initiated an investigation into illicit activity—including government hacking and surveilling—on Shakarami's Instagram account after her disappearance.

"We will rain those bullets down on you. You just wait."
Hadis Najafi, twenty-two-years-old, loved TikTok and Instagram. To her, those digital portals connected her to the outside world in ways her parents

could never have imagined. Her videos, rarely political in nature, often consisted of dance routines to international pop music and Iranian singers or fashion displays to her thousands of followers. She worked by day as a cashier at a restaurant. On September 21, 2022, she took to the streets of Karaj, in north-central Iran, to protest the mandatory hijab. On her way to the demonstration, she recorded a video of herself on her phone where she talked about her hopes for a brighter future in Iran. "In the end, I'll be happy...when everything is changing."[120]

Hadis never made it home alive. She was shot dead by security officials at the protest. Six bullet wounds pierced her head, neck, heart and abdomen. Her lifeless body was in such bad condition that her relatives were prohibited from seeing her at the hospital. Her death was the result of the violent crackdown on protesters instigated by former Iranian President Ebrahim Raisi who at the time asserted that protests should be "dealt with decisively."

Still, despite the violence and death, the "Woman, Life, Freedom" protests persisted. Hadis' sister later took to Instagram to post a story about the regime's indiscriminate violence on protesters: "You bastards shot her in the heart...how many bullets did you need to kill a girl who only weighed ninety pounds? Whatever it takes, we will rain those bullets down on you. You just wait."[121]

CHAPTER 6
CREATIVE RESISTANCE IN MUSIC, ART AND DANCE

"Life is normal. A laborer's annual wage is worth a dinner abroad...
Life is normal. Some have to sleep in graves, others own ten high-rises...
In the age of science, women are beaten for their beauty, thrown in the back of a police van and taken to unnamed prisons.
Our shopping cart is empty, no more oil left to export.
The rest of the world shoots for the Moon and Mars, while we are in the abyss."
–Toomaj Salehi, rapper, 2021

In many ways, the sixty-fifth Grammy Awards, held on February 5, 2023 in Los Angeles, was a typically glamorous affair. Trevor Noah returned to host for the third time, a slew of famous artists—ranging from Lizzo and Harry Styles to Mary J. Blige and Stevie Wonder performed—and Beyonce dominated, becoming the most decorated musician in Grammy history. That year's awards did feature several new categories, including "Best Song for Social Change," presented by First Lady Dr. Jill Biden. When Dr. Biden announced that category's winner, Shervin Hajipour, he didn't race to the stage to recite the standard thank you list of supporters, record label, manager, and partners.

Hajipour was, in fact, over seven-thousand miles away, fresh out of prison, and banned from leaving Iran. He had won the inaugural award for a viral song that became the unofficial anthem of the "Woman, Life,

Freedom" protests. Unfortunately, becoming the voice of Iran overnight also caught the attention of Iranian authorities. So, instead of basking in the applause of music industry celebrities at the Crypto.com arena in California, Hajipour celebrated his Grammy win by posting two words, "We won," on his Instagram page.

Hajipour was twenty-five-years-old when he posted his song, *"Baraye"* ("For the Sake of") on Instagram.[122] At that point, he was already well known in Iran—not for recording albums or staging live concerts, which are heavily restricted in Iran—but for making it to the finals of an Iranian talent show contest. Called *Asr-e Jadid* (New Era), the TV series is effectively "Iran's Got Talent," featuring a panel of three male judges evaluating child singing prodigies, dance ensembles, Persian balladeers, and even a choreographed fight between an all-female ninja team.[123] Despite his appearance on one of Iran's most popular TV shows, Hajipour was still an obscure singer outside Iran in 2022; but by the end of 2023, Hajipour would make it on *Time*'s list of the 100 most influential people in the world.[124]

Appropriately, social media was not just essential to the distribution of Hajipour's anthem, but also its inception. Following Mahsa Amini's death, millions of Iranians had taken to Twitter to write why they were rising up against the Islamic Republic, beginning their tweets with the phrase "For the sake of." Hajipour's ballad was made up of twenty-nine of those tweets from Iranians who had grown tired of seeing their beautiful country spiral into economic and environmental disrepair after decades of government mismanagement and corruption, compounded by isolation from the global economy and an international pariah status.[125]

Even though the song was devoid of graphic language about defeating the enemy or sacrificing one's life for the homeland, it still struck a nerve. It was a love letter to Iran, encapsulating a longing for an ordinary life. Hajipour listed the most basic of freedoms Iranians were fighting for: to dance, to kiss a loved one in public and, ultimately, to be free to do what you want with your life.[126] Within two days of posting, the music video had amassed forty million views on Instagram and was liked one and a half million times, a feat made even more impressive given the near-total internet shutdown in Iran:

For dancing in the alleys
For the fear when kissing
For my sister, your sister, our sisters

For changing rotten minds
For the shame of poverty
For longing to live an ordinary life
For the dumpster-diving kid and their dreams
For this dictatorial economy
For this polluted air
For Valiasr and its dying trees
For Pirouz[127] and the possibility of his extinction
For the innocent stray dogs
For our non-stop tears
For the image of this moment repeating again
For the smiling faces
For students and their future
For this forced paradise
For the imprisoned experts
For the Afghan kids
For this list that goes on and on

For all of these meaningless slogans
For the collapse of feeble buildings
For the sake of peace
For the rising sun after these long nights
For anxiety and insomnia
For men, homeland, prosperity
For the girl who wished to be a boy
For woman, life, freedom
For freedom
For freedom
For freedom

The song also inspired other musicians to create their own protest tunes. Buoyed by Hajipour's resonant lyrics, Kurdish musician and songwriter Chia Madani released his own version of the song on October 9, 2022 to highlight the unspoken pain and suffering of minorities in Iran. Madani focused particularly on the oppression and dehumanization of the Kurds in Iran whose cultural and political aspirations have continued to be crushed by the Islamic Republic since 1979.

With thanks to dear Shervin with sweet words, with tender words who made the pains of the millions into a flying message

You in Tehran, I am in Bokan
In Mahabad, in Kermanshah
In Piranshahr, in Saqqez
In Sanandaj, Urmia and Khorasan

In Ilam, in Oshnavieh
In Bane, Sardasht and Kamyaran
In Divandarreh, Hawraman
In Negheda and Marivan

Let me also just as you did
Pour out some of my endless pain
To put in words just a fraction of what remains to be unsaid
* with due respect for all your pain but my wounds are older than yours*
deeper than yours in my heart there are thousands "For"s
for the Jina's who are not allowed neither in life nor after death to be called
with their own names nor referred in history with that
for all mothers who had to wash their bullet riddled children with nothing
but rivers of tears
for all the Kurdish fathers asked to pay the cost of the bullet used to execute
their child just for asking their basic rights

For the teachers, for students
For all the broken pencils

For all the sighs full of longing
For an imprisoned language

For all those poems and books
Torn to pieces and forbidden
For all those cheerful songs
Now drenched in deep sorrow

For all those born as refugees, far from home
For those who will never return, for those who can never return

For Kurds, for Lors, Arabs, Baluchis
For all the peoples without rights
For centuries of oppression, of submission
For cultures and identities buried alive

Let's now write this yet once again
With my pains also visible
This time let's make sure your freedom aspires to set all of us free[128]

By mid-2023, as Islamic Republic security forces intensified their crackdown on street protests, Iranians sought creative new avenues to express dissent. In fact, music and dance soon became valiant acts of defiance because they were often seen as more dangerous in the eyes of the regime thanks to their potential for virality throughout Iran and abroad. Soon, government forces would declare war on the arts, music and dance—or "synchronized movement" as some regime officials called it—and, effectively, on the collective expression of dissent of millions of citizens. Never before had so many young Iranians been in sync to defy the regime, singing Shervin Hajipour's protest song *"Baraye."*[129]

The Ekbatan Girls Rise Up

In contrast to Hajipour's stitched-together laments of protesters, Rema and Selena Gomez's 2022 hit song "Calm Down" hardly had any revolutionary ambitions. But the mid-tempo pop song—featuring lyrics like "Girl, you sweet like Fanta"—set off a dance craze in Iran that had authorities worried. On March 8, 2023, five teenage girls shared a forty-second TikTok video of themselves in front of a nondescript tower block in Tehran's Ekbatan neighborhood, a planned community of 1970s high-rises. The teens, who became known as the "Ekbatan Girls," marked International Women's Day by dancing in sync to "Calm Down," with their hair uncovered, and wearing crop tops—three behaviors considered illegal for women in Iran.

In an instance of history rhyming, the Ekbatan video was recorded the same day that, in 1979, 100,000 women had gathered in Tehran's streets to vocally protest the mandatory hijab policies that the then-nascent Islamic Republic had imposed on women. Female resistance to the regime's conservative dress codes had persisted, but adapted over forty-six years. Now, the protest dance of a few teenage girls was seen by millions of people around the world. Women and girls were, again, proving to be a thorn in the side of the Islamic Republic. Unfortunately, the Iranian state's decades-old response to such dissent repeated itself, as well. Security forces tracked down the teenage girls to western Tehran and detained them for forty-eight hours, until the dance troupe published a forced apology.[130]

Iranian authorities could detain the creators of the video, but after the "Calm Down" dance went live, they couldn't contain what followed: a spontaneous eruption of dance in the streets of Iran by men, women and youth. If Iranians couldn't protest for their rights, they would dance and sing until they were free, despite it being illegal since 1979 for a woman to sing alone in public.

Selena Gomez threw in her support for the Iranian women dancing for their rights. "These young women and all the women of Iran who continue to be courageous [are] demanding fundamental changes," wrote Gomez in an Instagram story to her more than 400 million followers. "Please know your strength is inspiring."¹³¹

Iranian celebrities and human rights activists caught on to the dance trend, republishing videos of the Tehrani five dancing freely to "Calm Down." Actress and activist Golshifteh Farahani reposted the clip to her sixteen million followers on Instagram, adding the caption: "Nothing can stop women of Iran to be free. Nothing can stop all humans to be free."¹³² The clerical establishment, seeing a flood of illicit dancing in the street by unveiled women, was anything but calm, particularly as the "Calm Down" episode came on the heels of another high-profile video defying the Islamic Republic's constrictive controls on behaviors.

The Dance of the Influencers

A month before the five teenagers had kicked off a global sensation, Instagram influencers Astiyazh Haghighi and her fiancé, Amir Mohammad Ahmadi, both in their early twenties, posted a video of themselves. The glamorous couple, who between them have more than one million followers, had often posted videos showcasing advice for fans, their relationship, as well as routines of them dancing together. Haghighi's posts on Instagram also appeared to be pushing the strict boundaries of female dress, with her hair often only partially covered.¹³³ However, this video was a step too far for authorities. Haghighi and Ahmadi posted a video of themselves dancing together in front of the Azadi ("Freedom") Tower in downtown Tehran. To compound their noncompliance, Haghighi's long blonde hair was also uncovered.¹³⁴

Both influencers were reportedly beaten as they were arrested, tried without lawyers present, after which they were ultimately banned from leaving the country, and sentenced to five years in prison on charges of inciting anti-government protests. *Mizan Online*, a news outlet closely affiliated with the Islamic Republic's judiciary, invoked charges including "propaganda against establishment" and "colluding against national security."¹³⁵ Not only were the charges spurious, but the severity with which they described a brief public dance between an engaged couple was telling, demonstrating the Islamic Republic's disdain for any creative expression, particularly involving women.

It turned out that Haghighi, like Amini, already had a confrontation with Iranian security forces after being detained by morality police in September 2022 for "inappropriate" clothing. "They took me inside the van…the fear that it had given me never left me," she said of one brush-up with the morality police in an Instagram post. Then, addressing her one million Instagram followers directly, she exclaimed: "You often curse me, asking why I don't speak up. I want to tell you that I can't, not because I don't want to. It's because my mother has no one but me, and I am the head of the family."[136]

Haghighi had good reason to suspect that her followers wanted more vocal advocacy from her. As weeks of protest wore on—and with no structured organization or opposition leadership figure to rally around—Iranians increasingly turned to movie stars, singers, artists, sporting legends, and other cultural icons to use their elevated platforms to voice support for the protests and build momentum. But, as Haghighi's punishment showed, Iranian authorities recognized the dangers of artistic protests and intensified their crackdowns even on high-profile figures. The Islamic Republic made clear to prominent figures that they were not immune to the government's wrath. Failure to stay out of political matters, whether a celebrity or not, could result in a death sentence.

Instead of serving her full sentence, Haghighi left Iran for good. An October 28, 2023 Instagram post showed her at an airport with her mother with the message in Persian: "Sometimes destiny takes you with it and you have no choice. The only one I have left. Forced."[137] Since then, and having settled down in Istanbul, her posts have shown Iranians the freedom she enjoys in other countries.

Rap From the Rat Hole

Before the "Woman, Life, Freedom" protests erupted, Iranian rapper Toomaj Salehi, who is a member of the Bakhtiari minority group, had already faced the government's wrath for his political stances. He had been imprisoned for over a year—and at one point faced the death penalty—for using his music to allegedly orchestrate an "armed and group rebellion against the regime."[138]

Salehi's lyrics encapsulated with powerful brevity the frustrations and helplessness Iran's young generation had felt for far too long. Videos on his Instagram page also showed him standing side-by-side with demonstrators, encouraging them to protest on the streets of Iran. For Salehi, rap was an act of rebellion, and one of the few remaining vehicles available to those across Iranian society—rich or poor—to express themselves, an artistic expression of dissent described by Salehi as "the voice of suffocated throats."[139]

The lyrics of Salehi's first hit song, *Rat Hole* ("*Soorakh Moosh*"), released in late 2021, landed him front and center of the Islamic Republic's censorship machine. "Buy yourself a rat hole," he rages at the clerical elite but also at those in positions of influence who stood idly by as the government repressed its own people:

> *If you saw people's pain but looked away,*
> *If you saw the oppression of the innocent and ignored it,*
> *If you did it out of fear or for your own personal interests,*
> *You're the oppressor's accomplice,*
> *And you're also a criminal.*[140]

A week before he was arrested in his home in Isfahan on October 30, 2022, Salehi released a music video, *Omen* ("*Faal*"), where he makes bold predictions about the future of the Islamic Republic's regime as it continues to brutalize the country's citizens. "How many young people did you kill to build towers for yourself?" the rapper lyricizes. "Someone lost their young children and someone has lost their youth. Another's crime was having hair flow freely in the wind," he sings. "Another person's crime was being brave and having a sharp tongue."

In the music video, Salehi reads the patterns left in his white espresso coffee cup as a metaphorical prognostication of what lies ahead for the Islamic Republic and how the people of Iran would not be beaten into submission. Salehi lays blame not just at the regime for its brutality but also at ordinary Iranians who stand idly by, or acquiesce, without standing up to injustice. "I saw a cage in the coffee grounds—a lion hunting a jackal," he sings, alluding to a storied fable about wisdom ultimately triumphing over brute strength.[141] "We will rise from the bottom and target the top of the pyramid," Saleh sings, envisioning a future Iran where the clerical establishment is defanged and freedom-seeking citizens thrive in peace and prosperity.

Your whole past is dark
The government that took the light out of the eyes
I see a river in the future
I see prosperity and building
I see people who are happy
//
I see your money has no power anymore
Weapons no longer work for you
Both your unimportant people and your bosses are arrested

Toomaj was charged with spreading "corruption on Earth" and shortly afterwards a video circulated online showing a blindfolded man, believed to be the dissident rapper, expressing regret for his fiery words and confessing to his actions—both of which are common outcomes in the Islamic Republic following prolonged interrogations, physical torture and psychological abuse. In August 2024, Salehi's death sentence was overturned by the Iranian Supreme Court and he was cleared of his original conviction. He remained behind bars until December 1, 2024,[142] after being convicted of publishing erroneous statements on social media and for disrupting public order.[143]

On December 17, 2022, Iranian actress Taraneh Alidoosti became another celebrity to find herself in the Islamic Republic's crosshairs. Alidoosti, who starred in the Oscar-winning 2016 film *The Salesman*, had committed an increasingly common crime following Amini's death: posing for a photo on Instagram without a hijab in support of the "Woman, Life,

Freedom" movement. In response, she was arrested in her Tehran home and sent to the notorious Evin Prison, where she was held for nineteen days.

A week before her arrest, Alidoosti had also written to her millions of followers on social media about the unjust death sentence handed to twenty-two-year-old Tehrani barista Mohsen Shekari on December 8, 2022, who was hurriedly executed by the state for the all-encompassing crime of "enmity against God" and "corruption on Earth."[144] "His name was Mohsen Shekari," Alidoosti wrote. "Every international organization who is watching the bloodshed and not taking action is a disgrace to humanity."

Visual Art

While much of the creative protest was rooted in popular music, dance, and online culture, Iranian protest art, in the form of paintings, sculptures, installations, murals, posters or street art, also played an important role in energizing the "Woman, Life, Freedom" protests. These creators were joining a long history that dates back to hieroglyphics being used to criticize ancient Egyptian pharaohs to artists in ancient Greece using their tools to challenge conventional political and social norms of the day.[145] When words fall short—or are silenced—art is a powerful social and political tool to drive change. Since Mahsa Amini's death, Iranians inside Iran and abroad have resorted to the powerful medium of art to express their hopes and fears.

Artists draw from their lived experiences and trauma, says Parastou Forouhar, an Iranian artist and activist now living in Germany. Her parents, Dariush and Parvaneh, were high-profile political activists who were stabbed to death in their Tehran homes in November 1998. "Every act of resistance is a spark of hope," she said. "In my work, I use the image of a butterfly. It is a magical creature, as thin as paper, with so many patterns. It has a poetic role in Iranian literature, and in other cultures—in Greece it represents the soul. It's a symbol of resurrection, and it's also my mother's first name, Parvaneh."[146]

Weeks after Mahsa Amini's death, in late September of 2022, an anonymous artist, drawing on the trauma and anger felt by vast swathes of the Iranian population, dyed a fountain blood red outside the Artists Forum at Tehran's Honarmandan Park to highlight the Islamic Republic's violence and repression toward its people.

In late 2022, Iranians and other activists also used art to spread an important message outside of Iran, as well. On December 14, 2022—three months after Amini's death—the United Nations' Economic and Social Council (ECOSOC) met to vote on a U.S.-drafted resolution to expel the Islamic Republic from the forty-five-member Commission on the Status of Women (CSW). The measure was backed by Vice President Kamala Harris who released a statement on November 2 saying, "The United States continues to stand with the brave women of Iran as they protest peacefully for their fundamental rights and basic human dignity," adding that, "Iran has demonstrated through its denial of women's rights and brutal crackdown on its own people that it is unfit to serve on this Commission."[147]

Ahead of the vote, the activist/artist collective "For Freedoms," teaming up with Iranian artists and "Vital Voices," a women's leadership empowerment NGO, convened to construct a memorable exhibit to remind the U.N.—and the world—what was unfolding in Iran. Over twenty-three days, the group had assembled "Eyes on Iran," a collection of art installations spread throughout the four-acre Franklin D. Roosevelt Four Freedoms State Park on Roosevelt Island, facing the United Nations across the East River waterfront.[148]

Among the artists and political figures who spoke at the installation's inauguration in late November 2022 was photographer and filmmaker Shirin Neshat, who said the artists featured in the exhibit were working "in solidarity with the courageous Iranians who are risking their lives to express their human rights." Tabriz-born brothers Saman and Sasan Oskouei, known professionally as Icy and Sot, laid out in a grid 648 bricks inscribed with names of protesters who had either been arrested or killed by Iran's security forces since the uprising first began. The installation, which the brothers called *Bricks of a Revolution*, symbolized "just a small fraction of those arrested during the revolution. These bricks represent the strength of the activists who are currently risking their lives, inside and outside of prison, to fight oppression." For Iranian-Greek artist Aphrodite Désirée

Navab's installation, *Uproot the Roots, Rise Up*, she affixed green bandanas with the word "*Zan*" (Woman) around the trunks of the park's trees.

The exhibit's centerpiece was a giant mural of an eye on the steps on the park, featuring the names in black Persian script of approximately 400 Iranian demonstrators killed or injured since Mahsa Amini's death set off mass protests in Iran. The visual of the eye was a message to the U.N. and the world to not take its eyes off the remarkable bravery of Iranians fighting for their freedoms. Speaking at the exhibit's opening ceremony and about the upcoming U.N. vote, Hillary Clinton said: "The fact that Iran is a member [of the Commission] is a bitter irony. What we are seeing is a revolution led by young women who are just not willing to live with the loss of freedom being imposed upon them."[149]

The vote ended up passing, with the Islamic Republic of Iran being removed from the Commission on the Status of Women for the remainder of its 2022-2026 term. Twenty-nine countries voted in favor, eight voted against—including Russia and China—and sixteen countries abstained. Speaking after the vote, U.S. Ambassador to the United Nations, Linda Thomas-Greenfield, said removing Iran was the right thing to do. "It's hugely important for the women of Iran," she said. "They got a strong message from the United Nations that we will support them and we will condemn Iran and we will not let them sit on the Commission for the Status of Women and continue to attack women in their own country."[150]

Like social media, art and other cultural expressions by Iranians not only added to the richness of the protest, but also kept it alive both inside and outside Iran. Because of the skill and passionate affinity that younger Iranians have for both social media, dance, music, and popular culture, they became important tools to wield against a regime that has a paranoid approach toward any kind of self-expression. The videos of girls dancing to Selena Gomez and their subsequent persecution, for example, cut through all the other news and noise to grab the attention of the world in a way that staid press releases or speeches by opposition groups never would. Even where the street protests were being silenced, social media, visual arts, music, and dance continued the revolution.

CHAPTER 7
THE DUEL IN DOHA

"Minutes before a match, the deputy chairman of the federation would constantly whisper in my ear to be careful not to let my head cover drop."[151]
—Parisa Jahanfekrian, Iranian former weightlifting champion, 2023

Mario Ferri is neither Portuguese nor Uruguayan. Yet the Italian activist and footballer for India's second-division club United Sports Club, stole the headlines during Portugal's 2-0 group stage victory over Uruguay at the 2022 World Cup in Qatar. Fifty minutes into the game, and with the scoreline still deadlocked at 0-0, Ferri jumped the barriers and ran onto the pitch of Lusail Stadium waving an LGBTQ+ flag and wearing a blue Superman T-shirt that bore the slogans "Save Ukraine" on the front and "Respect for Iranian Women" on the back. The crowd cheered and whistled before Ferri was tackled to the ground by two stewards and escorted off the pitch. The game's referee, Alireza Faghani, himself Iranian, then picked Ferri's rainbow flag off the ground and moved it to the sidelines for play to resume.

Ferri was subsequently detained by Qatari authorities and his *Hayya* card, the visa permitting him entry into the country, was revoked. Ferri later explained on Instagram why he interrupted play in Qatar in what he described as his "Last Dance." He wrote that he wanted to send the world a message "for Iran where I have friends who suffer, where women are not respected…THE WORLD MUST CHANGE. We can do it together with STRONG gestures, which come from the heart, WITH COURAGE."

The tournament in Qatar marked many firsts: the first World Cup held in the Middle East; the first to take place in a conservative Muslim country; the first time the quadrennial tournament occurred in November and December instead of the summer; and the first time the most-watched sporting event in the world was hosted around a single city, Doha.

Qatari officials saw the World Cup as an opportunity for the tiny petrostate to flex its cultural muscle on a global stage and foster tourism, foreign investment and, ultimately, further diversify its economy. To do so, they had spent twelve years and an unprecedented $300 billion preparing for showtime, including building seven new stadiums from scratch, as well as 100 hotels and an entirely new metro system. Perhaps as gratitude, the International Federation of Association Football, better known as FIFA, worked assiduously to mute any kind of politics from encroaching on the 2022 World Cup in the months leading up to the tournament. But, in just seconds, Ferri's pitch invasion had brought to the fore three deeply political realities that FIFA could not ignore: Russia's invasion of Ukraine in early 2022, the lack of LGBTQ+ rights in Qatar, and the ongoing protests in Iran.

In fact, the political drama around these games had begun well before the first game kicked off. For years, critics and pundits had accused Qatar of "sportswashing" as a way of distracting the world from its treatment of migrant workers, minorities, and LGBTQ+ individuals. Then, days before the tournament began, the Qatari monarchy decided to ban the sale of alcohol at all eight stadiums, much to the dismay of many of the approximately one million fans who had traveled to Qatar. The move also strained FIFA's long-running relationship with Budweiser, which forks out seventy-five million dollars every four years as a major tournament sponsor.

Nonetheless, FIFA went to great lengths to protect the host nation from its detractors. When diatribes against Qatar grew louder in the weeks leading up to the World Cup, particularly on the topic of the country's treatment of migrant workers and LGBTQ+ people, FIFA President Gianni Infantino responded with a seething statement, accusing the West of hypocrisy. "What we Europeans have been doing for the last 3,000 years...we should be apologizing for the next 3,000 years before starting to give moral lessons," he said.

Before the World Cup opening ceremony, FIFA also cautioned several European countries against wearing a "One Love" captain's armband featuring a multicolored striped heart. England captain Harry Kane had reportedly planned to wear the colorful armband—said to foster inclusivity for people of all sexual and cultural backgrounds—in his opening match against Iran, but ended up not doing so after FIFA warned that any player found promoting politicized messages on the pitch would be penalized with a yellow card.

FIFA's aggressive approach to policing armbands in turn led to the football governing bodies of England, Wales, Holland, Switzerland, Germany, Denmark and Belgium to issue a joint statement expressing their frustration. "FIFA has been very clear that it will impose sporting sanctions if our captains wear the [colorful] armbands on the field of play," the statement read. "As national federations, we can't put our players in a position where they could face sporting sanctions...We were prepared to pay fines that would normally apply to breaches of kit regulations and had a strong commitment to wearing the armband. However, we cannot put our players in the situation where they might be booked or even forced to leave the field of play. We are very frustrated by the FIFA decision which we believe is unprecedented...Our players and coaches are disappointed. They are strong supporters of inclusion and will show support in other ways."[152]

Adding to political tension, the Iranian squad had already taken a controversial public stand against their leadership in an international friendly match against Senegal a month before the World Cup kicked off. On September 27, 2022, about two weeks after the death of Mahsa Amini, Iran's players donned black jackets over their white kits in protest during the national anthem, which some players refused to sing. By then, Iran had already qualified for the World Cup, making it even harder for FIFA, Qatar, or any other body to completely silence political protest at the games.

Team Melli

Iran is a football-mad nation. It is by far the country's most popular sport, serving almost as the country's secular religion. Despite being part of a tough group in the World Cup alongside England, Wales and the United States—the only group where all teams were in the top twenty global FIFA rankings—hopes were high for the Iranian squad, known affectionately by fans as *Team Melli*, going into the tournament. In fact, Iran's 2022 World Cup squad boasted arguably its most talented roster to ever participate in a major international tournament. The "Brazil of Asia," as some Iranians described the team, included the likes of goalscorer Mehdi Taremi, who was playing for FC Porto at the time, silky center forward Sardar Azmoun, then playing for German club Bayer Leverkusen, and towering goalkeeper Alireza Beiranvand, who saved a memorable penalty kick from Cristiano Ronaldo at the previous 2018 World Cup in Russia. Veteran Portuguese boss Carlos Queiroz was the only manager in Iran's history to lead the nation to three consecutive World Cup tournaments.

Because of the importance of the World Cup within Iran, the Islamic Republic had also gone to great lengths to sanitize its country's participation in Doha. In coordination with the Qatari government, three reporters from the most prominent anti-government news outlet, *Iran International*—a Persian- and English-language news outlet headquartered in London—were prevented from freely covering the World Cup. Their entry permits to Qatar were delayed or declared invalid, and several *Iran International* reporters were threatened by government-linked news outlets about traveling to Qatar. *Farhikhtegan Daily*, a hardline national broadsheet, publicly threatened to kidnap *Iran International* journalists who reported negatively on the Islamic Republic while in Qatar.[153]

This was not, however, the first time that football and politics have become entwined in Iran. In 2006, Iran was even temporarily suspended from participating in international tournaments by FIFA after former President Mahmoud Ahmadinejad was accused of instructing his government to meddle in the national team's affairs with the sacking of Mohammad Dadkan as President of the Iranian Football Federation.[154]

Even today, pledging loyalty to the clerical establishment is paramount in sport, while rejecting the state narrative can end an athlete's career.

In June 2022, Voria Ghafouri, the decorated captain of Esteghlal FC who has spoken out about civil rights abuses in Iran, was informed that his contract would not be renewed, infuriating fans who lambasted the decision as being political and not performance-related. In November 2022, state-run news agencies reported that Ghafouri, who was not selected to be in the Iran squad traveling to Qatar for the World Cup, had been arrested for "insulting the national soccer team and propagandizing against the government."[155]

The IRGC Stranglehold

Many years earlier, Sardar Pashaei, Iran's 1998 junior sixty-kilogram Greco-Roman world champion wrestler and national coach, had his eyes on gold at the Olympic Games in Sydney in 2000. When I interviewed Pashaei, he explained how after pre-qualifying, Iran's sporting authorities banned him from leaving the country because of his Kurdish origins and because his father had protested against the Islamic Republic when it formed back in 1979.[156]

Nine years later and still under pressure, Pashaei left Iran for America. Now residing in Virginia, Pashaei serves as a campaign manager at United for Navid, an action group that has set out to expose the murky relationship between Iran's sporting and political authorities. According to Pashaei, there is a revolving door between Iran's sports federation and the IRGC. One such example is Mohammad Reza Davarzani, who headed Iran's Volleyball Federation while also being a former IRGC commander embroiled in various corruption scandals.[157]

"These IRGC commanders wear suits instead of their army clothes and present themselves as sports people," Pashaei said, adding that part of his mandate at United for Navid involved contacting sporting authorities worldwide, including the International Olympic Committee, the World Karate Federation and FIFA, to raise awareness about the illicit politicization of sports in Iran.

United for Navid, consisting of exiled former wrestling, karate, judo and futsal champions, is named after Navid Afkari, a promising wrestler from Shiraz who was executed by the Islamic Republic on September 12, 2020 at the age of twenty-seven after taking part in anti-government protests that swept the country in 2018. Forced confessions released by the government purported to reveal that Afkari had allegedly attacked and killed a water company security employee amid the protests, although those close to him reject such claims.

Afkari's impending execution made international headlines, even prompting President Donald Trump to tweet: "To the leaders of Iran, I would greatly appreciate if you would spare this young man's life, and not execute him. Thank you!"[158] Those requests fell on deaf ears, and Afkari became yet another victim of a ruthless regime that arrests and executes political opponents, dissidents, athletes, ethnic minorities and journalists as a tool to instill fear and maintain power.

Two years later, and just two weeks before the World Cup kicked off, an accomplished karate champion, twenty-two-year-old Mohammad Mehdi Karami, became another athlete to suffer at the hands of Iranian security forces attempting to smother protest. Karami, arrested in connection with the killing of a *Basij* officer in the city of Karaj, was tried and convicted in approximately fifteen minutes without access to a lawyer of his choosing.[159] After his sentencing, Mohammad called his father, Mashallah Karami, a street vendor, to deliver a message: "Dad, they gave us the verdict," he said, in tears. "Mine is the death penalty. Don't tell mum anything."[160]

Hanged on January 7, 2023, his death was a chilling reminder of the risks athletes face for speaking out against the government.

#BlueGirl

Another victim of the regime's restrictive policies is Iranian futsal player Shiva Amini, who in 2009 was prohibited from competing professionally in Iran after being photographed unveiled while playing futsal abroad with some boys in Zurich. "We must follow the rules of the government, otherwise we'll be excluded from sports and society," she said.

When Amini called the Iranian Football Federation to dispute her ban, she was accused of fraternizing with a foreign enemy. "Another law that hinders the progress of women in Iran is the fact that they need permission from men to leave the country," she said.[161] Amini had built a good life in Iran, owning a house and a car, but she knew she would be arrested if she tried going back to her family in Isfahan. "If I went back to Iran now, they would arrest me in the airport. They would kill me because they are against girls, especially girls who speak out, who fight them. The Islamic Republic took everything from us, except hope. Now I'm fighting against them. In Iran, a girl has no rights. She cannot ride a bicycle, or go to a stadium."[162]

Iran does send female footballers like Shiva Amini abroad, but in 1981, Iranian female fans were banned from entering stadiums to watch men's football matches across the country. In 2018, Saudi Arabia lifted its country-wide ban on women attending men's matches, leaving Iran alone with Taliban-run Afghanistan as one of the few countries in the world where women's spectator rights are severely restricted.

For many Iranian sports enthusiasts, including Sahar Khodayari, watching their beloved sports team from the stands was a distant hope. In March 2019, Khodayari, attempted to sneak into Azadi Stadium in Tehran disguised as a man to watch her favorite team, Esteghlal FC, play against Al Ain FC from the United Arab Emirates. Despite its name, meaning freedom in Persian, the stadium was anything but free to women. Khodayari was arrested by security officials for not wearing a hijab in public and sentenced to six months in jail. Outside on the steps of the courthouse on September 2, 2019, she set herself on fire and later died in hospital with severe burns covering 90 percent of her body.

Condemnations swept the internet as news of Khodayari's death spread. She was quickly dubbed the "Blue Girl," based on the team color of the Esteghlal squad and the hashtag, #BlueGirl, spread on social media, calling to attention Iran's draconian ban on female sports spectators. Esteghlal F.C.'s English-language Twitter account posted a photo of Khodayari in hospital, her face and body covered in bandages, with the caption:

"Our dear Sahar burnt herself to death, when she was charged to six months in jail for...going to the stadium to support her #Esteghlal. She supported us despite the politics making it illegal for her, but what can we do to support her? ABSOLUTELY NOTHING. We are cowards."

Several members of Sweden's national women's team expressed their outrage at Khodayari's death. "This is a tragedy and it can't continue anymore," Kosovare Asllani, the team captain, posted on Twitter. "@FIFA, it's time to act and not be silent. WE need to help the women of Iran fight against gender apartheid. This is about human rights! #SaharKhodayri."[163]

"What happened to Sahar Khodayari is heart-breaking and exposes the impact of the Iranian authorities' appalling contempt for women's rights in the country," decried Amnesty International's Middle East and North Africa Research and Advocacy Director, Philip Luther. "Her only 'crime' was being a woman in a country where women face discrimination that is entrenched in law and plays out in the most horrific ways imaginable in every area of their lives, even sports...This discriminatory ban must end immediately and the international community, including football's world governing body, FIFA, and the Asian Football Confederation, must take urgent action to end the ban and to ensure that women are allowed access to all sports stadiums without discrimination or risk of prosecution or punishment."

In October 2022, a month before the World Cup kicked off, Spanish law firm Ruiz-Huerta & Crespo, representing former and current Iranian sports figures, sent a letter to FIFA urging the governing body to remove the Islamic Republic of Iran from the competition, in large part due to the regime's discriminatory practices toward women. "Football, which should be a safe place for everyone, is not a safe space for women or even men," the letter stated. "Women have been consistently denied access to stadia across the country and systematically excluded from the football ecosystem in Iran, which sharply contrasts with FIFA's values and statutes." A press release distributed alongside the letter added: "Iran's brutality and belligerence towards its own people has reached a tipping point, demanding an unequivocal and firm disassociation from the footballing and sports world."[164]

Though barring female spectators from entry contravened FIFA's policies on equality, the organization had either ignored the Iranian ban or made weak efforts toward convincing the Iranian government to remove it, mirroring the ineffectiveness of other international organizations and governments when confronting Iran on human rights matters.

In late 2023, however, female fans were finally allowed into stadiums. Such was the case in December 2023, when 3,000 women were permitted entry to the upper tiers of Tehran's Azadi Stadium to watch the capital's derby between Persepolis and Esteghlal.[165] The move, certainly a step forward from the total ban on female fans, hardly amounts to "equality" as women's attendance is capped at 3 percent of the total stadium's capacity, with the gender segregated areas often having the worst views of the field.[166]

A Secret Boxer
Like many other athletes who fell afoul of the Islamic Republic, Sadaf Khadem didn't grow up with political ambitions. Her goal was to become Iran's first female boxing champion, although female boxing is banned. (In fact, for twelve years after the Islamic Revolution, boxing for men was temporarily banned as it was considered an overtly American sport.)[167] In her teens, Khadem would train in public parks, or discreetly in boxing rings dressed in men's apparel so as not to arouse suspicion about her gender, letting her boxing prowess and work ethic do the talking in the ring.

On April 13, 2019, Khadem got her big break when she became the first female Iranian boxer to fight in France. The fight was scheduled in the southwestern coast city of Royan in front of 1,500 spectators, but French secular laws meant she had to fight with her hair uncovered. Khadem won the fight. Three days later, she received death threats from the Islamic Republic.

Khadem decided to remain in France, where she lives and trains. "The forced exile was only for a year and, after that, it was I who chose to stay in

France," Khadem said. "I am not saying that it is paradise [in France] ...but compared to a country like Iran, I am freer."[168]

Since Mahsa Amini's death, Khadem has taken the fight outside the ring, becoming more vocal about the Islamic Republic's brutality. "It is not ok to kill people in 2022, whether men or women, for a piece of clothing," she said. "I don't accept this and I fight for human rights. It pains me that people are protesting [in Iran] and the price that they are paying is their lives. People are protesting for democracy, to have a country where they can live more freely."

For Khadem, her boxing journey is not just a pursuit to sporting greatness, but a message to the people of Iran of what freedom looks like. "If I don't speak up today, I will regret it tomorrow. I stand by the Iranian people until the day Iran becomes free. I am their soldier. I am a champion in the eyes of the Iranian people. I stand by them until the end for freedom and for human rights."[169]

Game One: Iran v. England

Back in Qatar at the 2022 World Cup, Iran was thumped by England in their opening game, 6-2. However, global headlines focused on the many forms of political protest that exploded during the match. Droves of Iranian supporters in the stands brandished signs bearing the unofficial "Woman, Life, Freedom" slogan of the anti-government protests. Other fans waved Iran's pre-revolution lion and sun flags, another motif of anti-government revolt. Given the controversy around women being banned from Iran's stadiums—a policy that came into effect shortly after the 1979 revolution—even the sight of groups of Iranian women together in Khalifa International Stadium was significant. Even more shocking, though, was the silence of the crimson-clad Iranian national team who, on opening day and in front of a global audience, refused to sing the country's national anthem.

Before the tournament, team manager Carlos Queiroz had been explicit that his players were "free to protest." The country's captain and left-back, Ehsan Hajsafi, recognized the dissent brewing among the Iranian population, saying: "We have to accept that the conditions in our country are not right and our people are not happy." So, in a show of support for the Iranians protesting against the theocratic gerontocracy in Tehran, the team simply refused to sing the song which had been adopted in 1990 after the death of Supreme Leader Ruhollah Khomeini. The deafening silence of the players was coupled with spectators in the stands who whistled and booed in an attempt to drown out the music of the anthem. Shortly after the final whistle blew in Iran's embarrassing defeat to England, Yahya Golmohammadi, a former national team captain and coach, tweeted that the game's outcome was "God's punishment."

Back in football-mad Iran, there was an unusual range of reactions toward the Iranian national team. Some applauded the squad's gesture of support for the protests back home while others expressed their displeasure at some of the players' alleged links to the regime. Of particular concern to some fans was a meeting the national team had with President Ebrahim Raisi, a hardline cleric close to Supreme Leader Ali Khamenei, in Tehran days before the squad departed for Qatar. At the meeting, two players—Rouzbeh Cheshmi and Alireza Beiranvand—were photographed bowing deferentially to the president. Many cheered their national team's World Cup defeat as a way of demonstrating how committed their opposition to the government was. On the streets of Iran, protesters lit *Team Melli* banners alight, while chanting calls to boycott a team they felt had become too sympathetic to the regime.

Across the country, fans were divided about whether supporting their national team was a source of pride and unity, or if it was a distraction. Or worse, a way to divide a country already engulfed in mass unrest. "There's no honor in this," Farideh, a sixty-one-year-old mother of four, told the *LA Times*. "Many innocent people have been killed. Our children are suffering: *Team Melli* shouldn't have honored the Islamic Republic's flag."[170]

Legendary Iranian players, including Ali Karimi and Ali Daei, also weighed in, becoming among the first to support the "Woman, Life, Freedom" protesters and condemn the Iranian national team. Daei, one of the most prolific international goal scorers in history, also rejected an ambassadorial invitation by FIFA to attend the tournament in Qatar in favor of standing in solidarity with Iranian protesters. "I rejected the official invitation of FIFA and Qatar Football Federation to attend the World Cup with my wife and daughters," he wrote on Instagram. "I prefer to be next to you in my homeland and express my sympathy with all the families who lost loved ones over these days," he added, speaking directly to Iranian protesters back home. Daei was not imprisoned, but his passport was subsequently revoked for his vocal support for the protest movement.

Game Two: Iran v. Wales

A very different Iran national team lined the Ahmad Bin Ali Stadium for the second group stage match against Wales. After the team's defeat to England, and their silent protests during the national anthem, the players had been called to an urgent meeting with members of the Islamic Revolutionary Guard Corps—a clear sign that their protest on the biggest stage in world sports was seen as threatening and unacceptable by leadership back in Tehran.

During the tense meeting, the Iranian players were strongly encouraged to sing the national anthem, and to refrain from any sign of support for the political protests against the Islamic Republic. If they did continue to defy the regime, the IRGC made clear, their families back home would face repercussions. There were reports that the Iranian government had also dispatched thousands of regime sympathizers masquerading as fans to the Wales game to outnumber, out-chant and intimidate the dissenting Iranian spectators.[171]

Qatar also played a supporting role in Iranian political repression. Outside the stadium, an Iranian named Kiana Amirehsani was accosted by Qatar's uniformed "Tournament Security Force" for wearing a white T-shirt showing Mahsa Amini's face and the words "Woman, Life, Freedom" emblazoned in English and Persian. The security force informed her that she had to change her top before entering the stadium. When Amirehsani responded that she had no other shirt, they replied: "Go to the mall." Her brother, Kevin Amirehsani, who was filming the incident, pointed out that "the same T-shirt was worn at the last match, at the Iran-England match."[172] The siblings were eventually allowed to watch the game after agreeing to wear a different Iran football shirt and depositing her Mahsa Amini top, and two pre-1979 Iran flags, in lockers.[173]

The Iranian squad went on to bellow out the words of their anthem as well as defeat a lackluster Wales squad, 2-0, but their political ambivalence remained. When Ramin Rezaeian netted his first World Cup goal against the Welsh, in the 101st minute of play, he said he didn't know "whether to laugh or cry." Scoring on football's ultimate stage is a crowning achievement for any professional. But the Iranian players also knew that their victory was a pyrrhic one, and would be used as propaganda by a regime hoping to draw attention away from the tens of thousands of Iranian protesters back home, many of whom were being arrested, assaulted, tortured, and executed.

Game Three: Iran v. U.S.A.

Iran's third game of the group stage—and its last chance to advance to the knockout stages—came against the United States. Over the past half century, it would be hard to find a national relationship with more enmity than that of the United States and the Islamic Republic. On November 5, 1979, one day after a group of Iranian students seized control of the U.S. embassy in Tehran, Khomeini had referred to the United States as "The Great Satan." On January 29, 2002, President George W. Bush returned the favor, referring to Iran as part of an "Axis of Evil." For decades, official relations between the two nations didn't veer much from these absolutist terms.

Prime Minister Mosaddegh's ousting by the CIA and MI6, the U.S. embassy hostage crisis of 1979-1981, Iraq's invasion of Iran in 1980, the Iran-Contra scandal of 1985-1987, and President Trump's "maximum pressure" campaign of abandoning the Iranian nuclear deal and reimposing aggressive economic sanctions against Iran—all were key milestones in the precipitous deterioration of U.S.-Iranian relations. Now, in the midst of fierce street protests at home, the Iranian team lined up against the U.S., with a chance to advance to the next stage of the tournament—a feat the football-mad nation had never achieved.

There was also a precedent for this match. Going into the U.S. game, *Team Melli* had recorded just three victories in seventeen World Cup appearances. But their first-ever win had been unforgettable: a 2-1 victory over the U.S. at the 1998 World Cup in France. At that match, the Iranian team presented their U.S. counterparts with white roses and posed for a group photo together, but the Iranian team received strict orders from its government not to shake hands with the Americans. The match-up had been so politically contentious that even Supreme Leader Khamenei stayed up past his bedtime to watch his nation defeat "the Great Satan." After the game, Khamenei invited the scorer of the first goal, Hamid Estili, to his grand residence and kissed him on the forehead. Nearly twenty-five years later, on November 29, 2022, with the U.S. and Iran locked in a stalemate over nuclear negotiations and with anti-government protests convulsing Iran, it would have been nearly impossible to hide the political tensions as game time approached at Doha's Al-Thumama stadium.

Extra security personnel patrolled outside the stadium, confiscating paraphernalia from fans that betrayed support for the Iranian protest movement. Before kickoff, Iran's state media called for the U.S., their geopolitical and sports rival, to be booted from the World Cup after the U.S. Soccer Federation temporarily altered Iran's flag on its social media pages by removing the Islamic Republic symbol, in an apparent show of support for the women in Iran who were fighting for basic human rights. A spokesperson for the U.S. team later confirmed that the Islamic Republic's flag had been doctored intentionally.

"By posting a distorted image of the flag of the Islamic Republic of #Iran on its official account, the #USfootball team breached the @FIFAcom charter, for which a 10-game suspension is the appropriate penalty," wrote *Tasnim News Agency*, a media outlet linked to the Islamic Revolutionary Guard Corps. The tweet ended with the charge that "Team #USA should be kicked out of the #WorldCup2022."

Instead, it was Iran who left the tournament, with a first-half strike by U.S. talisman Christian Pulisic enough to seal a momentous 1-0 American victory. *Team Melli's* loss dominated the front pages of Iran's reformist and conservative newspapers. Conservative daily *Abrar-e Varzeshi* mourned that "The Wish was Lost." *Javan*, a daily newspaper with ties to the IRGC, adopted a more creative interpretation of Iran's loss, noting that the team "won the real game: the game of uniting people's hearts."[174]

The popular response was somewhat different. Though football is by far the country's most popular sport, many Iranians back home reveled in Iran's defeat to the United States. As soon as the final whistle was blown against the U.S. in Qatar, videos proliferated on social media of people throughout Iran celebrating *Team Melli's* loss, tooting their car horns, cheering, singing and, remarkably, waving U.S. flags. In Mahsa Amini's hometown of Saqqez, fireworks lit up the sky in celebration of Iran's defeat, a stark reminder of the disdain many Iranians protesting at home held for their government. Iranian protesters saw the defeat in Qatar as a mini victory that catapulted their grievances onto the world stage.

Nine members of Iran's squad played domestic football at that time and they were unlikely to receive a rapturous welcome home from the theocratic government, especially after that same squad took a stand by refusing to sing the country's national anthem at the beginning of the tournament. Iran's defensive midfielder Saeed Ezatolahi, who played club football in Denmark for Vejle Boldklub at the time, was reminded of the dire situation back home after his childhood team-mate, Mehran Samak, was shot dead by regime forces shortly after Iran's defeat to the U.S. Ezatolahi later wrote on Instagram in honor of Samak: "Someday the masks will fall, the truth will be laid bare…This is not what our youth deserve. This is not what our nation deserves."

Following Iran's politically-charged appearance in the World Cup, athletes continued to protest against the regime. Among them is Iranian chess master Sara Khadem, who competed in the FIDE World Rapid and Blitz Chess Championships in Kazakhstan in December 2022 without a head covering, and moved to Spain after an arrest warrant was issued against her in Iran. Despite not being allowed to return home, Khadem says she has no regrets. "I also decided to finally do something that I wanted to, to be myself," she said. "I was motivated by the people of Iran."[175]

CHAPTER 8
A DICTATOR'S DILEMMA

"We should try hard to export our revolution to the world, and should set aside the thought that we do not export our revolution, because Islam does not regard various Islamic countries differently and is the supporter of all the oppressed people of the world. On the other hand, all the superpowers and all the powers have risen to destroy us. If we remain in an enclosed environment, we shall definitely face defeat. We should clearly settle our accounts with the powers and superpowers and should demonstrate to them that, despite all the grave difficulties that we have, we shall confront the world with our ideology."[176]
—Ayatollah Ruhollah Khomeini, first Supreme Leader of the Islamic Republic of Iran, 1980

On May 19, 2024, the sun shone on Iran's president, Ebrahim Raisi, as he disembarked from an Iranian Air Force helicopter in northwestern Iran, near the Azerbaijani border. He was meeting with Azerbaijan's president, Ilham Aliyev, to celebrate their nations' cooperation in building the large Qiz-Qalasi dam. After posing for photographs, Raisi, flanked by his foreign minister, Hossein Amir-Abdollahian, returned to the helicopter to head to Tabriz. Long world-renowned for its carpets and textiles, Tabriz is now a heavily industrialized city of 1.7 million people located just eighty miles south of the Qiz-Qalasi dam. But, despite the short distance, the terrain Raisi's three-helicopter convoy traveled over was mountainous, with heavy fog obscuring the hills.

Two of the three helicopters landed safely, but Raisi's Bell 212—manufactured in the United States and purchased by Iran in the 2000s—never arrived.[177] After an extensive search, the wreckage of the helicopter was found the following morning in the Dizmar forest in the East Azerbaijan province.[178] In addition to Raisi, the crash claimed the lives of Raisi's security detail, the pilots, Iran's Foreign Minister, the governor of East Azerbaijan province, and Tabriz's Friday prayer leader, who also served as the Supreme Leader's official representative in East Azerbaijan.

Following Raisi's death, Iran declared a five-day period of mourning, but news of his death left many Iranians in a more celebratory mood. Videos of fireworks lighting up the sky, including in Mahsa Amini's hometown of Saqqez, circulated on Telegram soon after the announcement that his helicopter had disappeared.[179] In response, police stationed prominently in public areas and warned people who appeared happy during the five-day mourning period that they were subject to arrest.[180]

Whatever emotions Iranians portrayed publicly, social media posts made it clear that Raisi's death would not make them forget his long, prominent role in Iranian state brutality toward political prisoners, protesters, and other groups seen as hostile to the Islamic Republic. Beginning in the 1980s, Raisi had served as a jurist whose harsh sentences earned him a reputation as a "hanging judge." Most prominently, he was one of the members of a panel that, in 1988, sentenced as many as 5,000 political prisoners to execution. The death sentences were so rapid-fire that, at their height, prisoners had to be driven to the gallows by the truckload, arriving every half-hour.[181] So, well before his deadly crackdown on the 2022-2023 "Woman, Life, Freedom" demonstrations, Raisi was known by the ominous sobriquet of "The Butcher of Tehran."

Further weighing down Raisi's legacy were widespread accusations of fraud in the 2021 election that had landed him the presidency. Relations between the previous president, Hassan Rouhani, and Ayatollah Khamenei had soured as the Ayatollah began to view Rouhani as insufficiently hardline. The 2021 election was widely seen as a sham orchestrated by Ayatollah Khamenei's retinue to replace Rouhani with a more compliant loyalist. That perception contributed to a massive drop in voter participation, from over 70 percent in 2017 to 49 percent in 2021.[182] Following Raisi's controversial election, the country experienced economic woes, including a plummeting currency.[183] But if Raisi couldn't improve the economy, force Western countries to remove economic sanctions, or earn democratic legitimacy, he seemed determined to tighten the screws on the things he could control: stepping up the repression of protesters and tightening enforcement of hijab laws.

Following Raisi's death, his vice president, Mohammad Mokhber, took over in an acting role until a new president was elected. The result of the June 28, 2024 election, however, came as a bit of a surprise, particularly at a time of high political tension. The new president, Masoud Pezeshkian, is considered a pragmatic reformist and less likely to tow the conservative hardline positions that Raisi supported. Instead, Pezeshkian had previously criticized the harsh treatment of protesters, publicly sought to revive cordial relations with Western nations—except Israel—and supported the rights of ethnic minorities. Compared to Raisi, Pezeshkian was markedly less ideologically conservative and less in sync with the conservative clerical establishment and Khamenei. Would the combined impact of the long-running "Woman, Life, Freedom" protests, Raisi's death, and an allegedly reform-minded new president finally herald a transition toward a more tolerant and less ideologically rigid Iran?

The Limitations of Power

From the moment he assumed the presidency, whatever plans Pezeshkian had for reforming the government—or how much latitude he would get in implementing those ideas—were immediately complicated by two factors. The most immediate was the ongoing dangerous conflict between Israel and Iran, including its proxies like Hamas, Hezbollah, and the Houthi rebels. Any attempt by Pezeshkian to bring Iran out of its diplomatic isolation by improving ties with the West and appealing for them to loosen sanctions was going to be a much tougher sell with Iranian rockets raining over population centers in Israel. Likewise, Israeli attacks on military targets in

Iran were going to make it harder for Pezeshkian to shore support from hardline conservatives for opening up to Western nations.

However, even if Pezeshkian had assumed the presidency in a calmer geopolitical moment, there would still be another, more fundamental, limitation on his capacity to transform the politics of the Islamic Republic. The Iranian president does not hold anywhere near the same sort of executive powers as presidents in the United States or other nations. Instead, as his title suggests, ultimate power rests with the Supreme Leader.

Iran's president is responsible for the day-to-day running of affairs, while the Supreme Leader serves as head of state and commander-in-chief, wielding authority over the national police, the morality police, the Islamic Revolutionary Guard Corps and its paramilitary wing, the Basij Resistance Force. In U.S. terms, the Iranian president's role is perhaps better understood as that of a cabinet-level administrator. While the secretary of the treasury, secretary of state, or attorney general all wield real power, they also serve at the behest of the head of state.

In the unlikely event that Pezeshkian forgot his place, a senior member of the Supreme Leader's office, Alireza Panahian, offered a reminder ahead of the 2024 election. As Panahian put it, the next president would have to be unambitious, predictable and be ready to "sacrifice themselves" for Khamenei. They would also need to recognize the limitations of their mandate as merely "the head of 300,000 bureaucrats."[184]

So, while Iran today does have an elected president, a legislative body—the *majlis*—and a judiciary, those branches of government barely serve as a check on the jurisdiction of the Supreme Leader. Rather than indicating fundamental shifts in the nation's direction, the election cycles offer the illusion of political competition in a fundamentally authoritarian system where ultimate power rests with one individual exempt from elections and unbound by public scrutiny. Through this lens, even Pezeshkian's election could be seen as little more than a cynical ploy. Though clearly not the conservative clerical establishment's preference, Pezeshkian could have been allowed to win the presidency as a kind of near-meaningless concession to popular discontent. But, in Iran, winning the presidency is not the same as being allowed to implement an agenda. That is the ultimate purview of the Supreme Leader.

The Khamenei Era

For almost four decades, Ayatollah Ali Khamenei has served as Supreme Leader of the Islamic Republic of Iran, a tenure that makes him the longest-serving head of state in the Middle East. Throughout his reign as the Islamic Republic's second Supreme Leader, Khamenei has essentially ruled by divine, incontestable right, wielding ultimate control over the country's political, economic, security, military, administrative, and cultural affairs.

He has managed to retain his power even as seven U.S. presidents came and went both by his explicit powers and more shadowy methods. For example, the Supreme Leader can appoint and dismiss the heads of various power centers, effectively giving him control over the military, judiciary, intelligence agencies, media and broadcasting, as well as the police and other domestic law enforcement bodies, including the morality police. He is also the commander-in-chief of all the armed forces, including the IRGC. Additionally, Khamenei controls the disbursement of billions of dollars in religious endowments known as *bonyads*. The *bonyads*, a kind of parallel financial system to the government, are responsible for a great deal of corruption, but provide the Supreme Leader with a direct personal patronage system with clerical and military kleptocratic elites, who often become quite wealthy from the endowments.[185]

Over the past ten years, the Khamenei-controlled IRGC has also rapidly expanded its role in the economy. "Ten years ago, the IRGC was controlling about 10-15 percent of the economy," explained Spain's former Ambassador to Iran Angel Losada, "Today they control 70 percent of the economy...They will never lose power as long as they control the economy."[186]

Khamenei's predecessor, Ayatollah Khomeini, had initiated the initial conservative prohibitions of behavior in Iran, when music and alcohol were banned, adultery and homosexuality punishable by death, and engagement of any kind with the West, particularly the "Great Satan," was heavily discouraged. However, in the early months of 2019, Khamenei set out on an ambitious project of his own that he heralded as the "Second Phase of the Islamic Revolution." With the Islamic Republic four decades old at the time, the Supreme Leader sought to embark on a "purifying" process that would yield a new generation of Khamenei absolutists—or the *"Javan va hezbollahi"* (young and hardline) class—who would be responsible for ensuring that the Supreme Leader's ultra-conservative ideology and system of government long outlived him.[187]

Raisi's controversial June 2021 election win to the presidency was a direct result of this project to consolidate power. For all presidential elections, candidates have to be vetted by the Guardian Council, a body effectively controlled by the Supreme Leader. In 2021, the council disqualified previous regime insiders, including former presidents Hassan Rouhani and Mahmoud Ahmadinejad. Rouhani and Ahmadinejad represented different political visions, but both were now deemed inadequately servile to execute Khamenei's manifesto.

According to Sanam Vakil, who serves as the director of Chatham House's Middle East and North Africa program, any hopes that Khamenei may allow change within Iran would be misplaced. "We have to assess Ali Khamenei for his track record. He is not a compromising individual." Vakil added that the Supreme Leader "is a man who is focused on conservative consolidation and transition of the Islamic Republic."[188]

While Khamenei's near absolute grip on power has remained firm for decades, swirling rumors of his declining health have initiated discussions around what succession might look like. In 2014, he was treated for prostate cancer. In the week preceding Mahsa Amini's death, Khamenei, who turned eighty-six in 2025, was under close observation after having surgery for a serious bowel obstruction.

Iran's March 1, 2024 elections for the Assembly of Experts, the eighty-eight-member body of hardliners sympathetic to Khamenei who are mandated to supervise the Supreme Leader and elect a new head of state when the time is right, fueled further speculation about whether the assembly was preparing for a leadership succession race for the country's highest office.

Before his death in May 2024, Raisi had been widely touted as a frontrunner for the supreme leadership. He had clearly proven himself to be an obedient apparatchik and enforcer of the conservative principles of the theocracy. Diplomatically, Raisi showed no signs of improving relations with the West, instead promoting ties with Russia and China. There would also be a precedent for his ascension to Supreme Leader. Khamenei himself had followed a similar path to his current role, serving as President from 1981 to 1989 before being elevated to the role of Supreme Leader after the death of the Islamic Republic's founding father, Ruhollah Khomeini. Finally, Raisi's pristinely manicured white beard, black robe and turban identified him according to Shia tradition as a descendant of the Prophet Mohammad, a sound choice for a possible third Supreme Leader to perpetuate the Islamic Republic's system of government. Raisi had also, reportedly, expressed interest in the position years ago, in 2017.[189] Because of his frontrunner status, Raisi's death may actually be more consequential in terms of the looming succession plans for the country's aging Supreme Leader. Presidents can, after all, be picked, dismissed, and overruled.

With Raisi gone, the shortlist of names floated to replace Khamenei diminished further. Among the most notable possible successors were former Supreme Leader Khomeini's son Ahmad, who died of heart disease in 1995; former head of the judiciary Ayatollah Mahmoud Hashemi Shahroudi, who died reportedly of a brain tumor in late 2018; and former President Ali Akbar Hashemi Rafsanjani, who died of heart complications in 2017, although extremely high levels of radiation were found in his body during the autopsy.[190] The best-known candidate left in the mix is Mojtaba Khamenei, the Supreme Leader's fifty-five-year-old second son of four. Mojtaba currently serves as head of the *Beit-e rahbar*, the Supreme Leader's office housing some 1,700 employees who run his schedule, public appearances and day-to-day affairs. He also appears to fit his father's vision of a revitalized Islamic Republic spearheaded by younger but extremely conservative men.

Because of the near absolute lack of transparency in the selection of the country's most powerful figure, observers tend to watch every possible sign carefully. With Mojtaba, there have been two major signals of his advance toward the top of Iran's power structure over the past three years. In 2022, *Rasa News Agency*, a regime-linked outlet focused on religious news, published a short article mentioning that he had ascended to the rank of Ayatollah, a prerequisite for assuming the role of the Supreme Leader.[191] Then, on September 22, 2024, Mojtaba announced that he was discontinuing his virtual seminary classes. Clerics rarely leave seminary duties unless they are very ill or about to take on a more significant responsibility.[192]

Also, as the Islamic Republic faces threats from within and abroad, Mojtaba is likely to be the leading candidate who has his father's ear. In 2024 alone, Raisi died in a helicopter accident, Hamas political chief Ismail Haniyeh was assassinated at the time of Pezeshkian's inauguration in Tehran, Iran launched direct ballistic missile attacks on Israel, Hezbollah's Secretary-General, Hassan Nasrallah, was assassinated, and Israel's Mossad was thought to have infiltrated much of Iran's security apparatus, while disabling much of its air defense systems. In response, Khamenei has winnowed down the number of advisors he has contact with.

Mojtaba is not the only candidate in the running, though. Other potential candidates include Alireza Arafi, a trusted advisor to Khamenei who serves as the second deputy chairman of the Assembly of Experts and is also a member of the Guardian Council.[193] A third candidate with similarly close ties to Khamenei is Hashem Hosseini Bushehri, who serves as the Secretary of the Supreme Council of Seminaries and is the first deputy chairman of the Assembly of Experts.[194]

Another dilemma facing Khamenei as he considers naming his successor is a historical lesson from the early days of the revolution. In 1980, soon after the revolution, Ayatollah Khomeini suffered a heart attack and a quartet of his well-placed followers, including Khomeini's son, ruled over Iran. In order to dissuade competition that might weaken the newly formed regime, they nominated a successor designate, Grand Ayatollah Hossein Ali Montazeri, an old follower of Khomeini's and a learned theologian with no discernible political ambitions. The designation of Montazeri, intended to deter competition to replace Khomeini as the Supreme Leader, backfired. News of his status brought about a kind of leadership crisis that Vladimir

Lenin termed "dual power." By creating an official alternative to the aging Khomeini, the regime encouraged elites to turn away from the current Supreme Leader to offer their allegiance to Montazeri. Ultimately, Montazeri was stripped of his position—which seemed to have been invented by the parliament in any event—in 1989, paving the way for Khamenei's rapid and unexpected rise.[195]

Now, Khamenei may be facing a similar problem. He wants to have his preferred candidate become successor, but he doesn't want to pre-emptively back a powerful rival who will undermine his own authority. In this world in which Khamenei sees enemies inside and outside, he may uniquely trust his son, Mojtaba.[196]

There are some stumbling blocks in the younger Khamenei's path, though. For one, many Iranians associate him with the harsh crackdowns during the 2009 protests. The younger Khamenei was targeted with chants like "Mojtaba, may you die and not become Supreme Leader!"

Another hurdle surfaced in 2022. As rumors about Mojtaba's ascension were building, an opposition politician asked Khamenei to confirm or deny that he would pass leadership down to family members.[197] For students of Iranian history, the reference would have been clear. Notions of hereditary succession and nepotism were a repugnant practice vilified among the early progenitors of the Islamic Republic as evocative of the "illegitimate" Pahlavi dynasty that Khomeini overthrew in the 1979 Islamic Revolution. Khamenei himself had publicly endorsed the principle that: "dictatorship and hereditary government are not Islamic."

Finally, in December of 2022, Mohammad Sarafraz—a Khamenei confidant and the former head of Islamic Republic of Iran Broadcasting (IRIB)—took the extremely rare step of publicly criticizing Mojtaba's role in the violent response to the "Woman, Life, Freedom" protesters: "The method Mojtaba Khamenei has chosen to rule is wrong. This method of putting pressure on the people and not paying attention to their political and economic demands and their legitimate freedoms will not work."[198]

Sarafraz himself recognized the unprecedented, and potentially fatal, nature of criticizing Khamenei's son, saying, "I know that some kind of incident may happen to me by saying these words. I have also written a will."¹⁹⁹ It was an extraordinary episode that suggested not all of the conservative clerics who run the selection process rallied behind the Supreme Leader's son.

As the real center of power in Iran, replacing a Supreme Leader is more likely to bring about significant changes in the country's system of governance than a new president, even one with a huge popular mandate. That said, the process for selecting a new supreme leader virtually guarantees that whomever replaces Khamenei will also be deeply conservative. Supreme Leaders are appointed by the Assembly of Experts, the membership of which goes through the Guardian Council, a group either directly or indirectly appointed by the Supreme Leader. So, as with the election of Pezeshkian, or any other reform-minded president, whomever replaces Khamenei as Supreme Leader of the Islamic Republic is also unlikely to dramatically change the course of politics in Iran.

None of this means that there is no hope for fundamental change in Iran. Today, the nation is virtually cut off from the West, engaged in direct and indirect war with Israel and the United States, and economically isolated. More importantly, large swathes of the population, particularly young people, women, key industry workers, and ethnic minorities, are manifestly unhappy with declining standards of living and repressive social policies. Iran's authoritarian theocracy has successfully maintained control of the nation for nearly a half century, but how much longer can it continue down this path? And what do the Amini protests tell us about the viability of such an approach?

Just be Happy and Listen to Music

On December 12, 2022, four days after the barista Mohsen Shekari's secretive execution in Tehran—which became infamous via social media—another twenty-three-year-old, Majidreza Rahnavard, was hanged. This particular execution took place 550 miles to the east of Tehran on a crane in Mashhad's main square, yet many of the other macabre details were all too familiar. Rahnavard had been denied a lawyer of his choosing in his trial, accused of stabbing to death two members of Iran's *Basij* force, summarily convicted, and sentenced to death. Twenty-three days after his arrest, at 4:00 a.m., Rahnavard was hanged with his hands and feet bound and a black bag covering his head. His family was not informed of his execution until after his death, when they were given the name of a cemetery and a plot number. Mahmood Amiry-Moghaddam, director of "Iran Human Rights," stated that Rahnavard's sentencing was based on "coerced confessions, after a grossly unfair process and a show trial."[200]

It was a singularly agonizing moment for Rahnavard's family, but one that had played out repeatedly across the nation. There was, however, one extraordinary moment in this hurried execution: Rahnavard's reaction, captured on a cell phone. As he headed to the gallows, blindfolded and flanked by two masked guards, Rahnavard was asked about his final wish. His reply, in a video that quickly spread on social media, was that he didn't want anybody to mourn his death, adding: "Do not read the Quran. Do not pray. Just be happy and listen to music."[201]

Few things secularize a society more than an aggressive, theocratic tyranny. After years of state repression, most notably in 2017, 2019, and 2022-23, it's less-than-surprising that support for Iran's theocracy has quickly eroded. Recently-leaked government survey data found that support for a separation between religion and state in Iran had more than doubled in just nine years, from 31 percent in 2015 to 74 percent in 2024. Rahnavard's last wish—to ignore religious rituals of mourning in favor of enjoying music—served notice to the Islamic Republic of a much bigger societal shift.

Spanish Ambassador Angel Losada also noticed a surprising lack of interest in religion among Iranians during his term in Tehran. "Iranian authorities called [the protests] a war on the hijab. But during my time in Iran, I realized that many of the people of Iran were not very religious. The regime does promote religion but ordinary civilians were quite secular. The mosques are not full. When you try to impose a religion, you have the inverse effect." Losada, who had previously served as Spain's Ambassador to Kuwait, saw a sharp difference in religious observation between the two Muslim nations. "In Kuwait, people go to mosque on Fridays. In Tehran, the city empties out and people drive out of the city." The result is that, on weekends in the capital of the Islamic Republic of Iran, the city of ten million people "is rather quiet. You don't feel religion."[202]

As with the heads of many other NGOs, "Iran Human Rights" director Amiry-Moghaddam insists that the thousands of state-sanctioned executions of protesters following arrest, forced confessions and kangaroo trials, constitute a "crime [that] must be met with serious consequences for the Islamic Republic."[203] With Iran already heavily sanctioned and diplomatically isolated, the most serious consequences for the regime's despotic violence will likely come from within. In fact, it's hard to see how the Islamic Republic can survive when over seven in ten people prefer a form of government in which religion doesn't supersede democratic governance. Of all the problems that Iran's conservative clerical establishment might want to avoid, a widespread collapse of support for a theocratic form of government has to be near the top of the list.

This is not the only significant problem facing Iran's leadership. The rapid movement away from theocracy has been accompanied by a plummeting faith in voter participation in Iran. These numbers are particularly significant given the much higher historical voter participation in the Islamic Republic. In the presidential election of 1980, following the revolution, a reported 67 percent of people voted. Though these numbers flagged in the late 1980s and early 1990s, in the twenty years between 1997 and 2017, participation stood between 60 percent to 85 percent.[204]

The 2020 parliamentary election, in which voter turnout stood at 42 percent, the lowest since 1979, was a stark turning point.[205] During the contested 2021 presidential election—which typically sees higher turnouts than parliamentary elections—Raisi won, but voter participation also slipped to 49 percent, a sign of widespread belief that it was a sham.[206] Of those that did vote, over 10 percent cast blank ballots, another sign of protest and lack of faith in the electoral system.[207]

On March 1, 2024, Iranians headed to the ballot boxes again to vote for members of Parliament. The notable result of the election was not the outcome, which was a foregone conclusion, but the record-low electoral participation. Ten hours into voting, turnout stood at 27 percent. Even after the polls were unexpectedly kept open for two additional hours, nationwide turnout finished at a historic low of 40.6 percent.[208] In Tehran, turnout stood at 24 percent. In an even worse sign for the regime, there were grassroots anti-voting campaigns. Using the hashtag "No way I'll vote," Iranians in Iran and in the diaspora campaigned to boycott the elections, or "selections" as some called it, alluding to the dearth of genuine reformists or even moderates running in the elections who were outside of the clerical elite. The lower participation rates suggested a deep cynicism toward the government, in large part because of the ever-widening gulf between the aging clerical government and the country's young, disillusioned population.

However, those boycotting the election also included older, prominent former politicians who abstained from voting in the elections. One former president, Hassan Rouhani, was barred from participating in the elections to the powerful Assembly of Experts on the grounds that he was too moderate.[209] Another reformist politician, Mohammad Khatami, who served as Iran's fifth President from 1997 to 2005, declared: "This time, I've resolved that if I can't directly impact people's lives, I'll stand in solidarity with the numerous disheartened individuals who harbor the belief, deep within, that if there's a path forward, it lies in reformation."[210] The lack of faith in the system was also apparent a few months later, in the early presidential election to replace Raisi. Participation plummeted to just under 40 percent, another all-time low.[211]

A Balancing Act

In one sense, the Mahsa Jina Amini protests followed a well-worn path. While the government attempted to head off the spread of protests with a combination of conciliatory statements and fabrications about the cause of, first, Amini's death, and then those of countless other protesters, even more violent forms of repression followed very quickly. Despite the unique elements of the protests—women-led, unification of ethnic minorities, more intense reliance on social media, and its systemic goal of removing the Supreme Leader and even the Islamic Republic itself—the successful, violent shutdown of street protests by early-to-mid 2023 was an eerily familiar result.

These are exactly the same tactics that the Islamic Republic has used to manage multiple widespread protests for over forty-six years. In doing so, the authorities have been brutally effective at squashing dissent. Under both Supreme Leaders, Ayatollah Ruhollah Khomeini and Ayatollah Ali Khamenei, Iran's governments have confronted protesters demanding change with intense repression, including militarized police, paramilitary forces, and sham trials followed by, to date, thousands of executions.

Iran's current government has managed to navigate, at least for now, what's known as "the dictator's dilemma," the balancing act that many authoritarian regimes face when dealing with popular unrest. If these regimes remain steadfastly hostile to change, the protests will continue to grow.[212] However, any concessions on their part may be interpreted as weakness, which could also galvanize protests. Earlier in Iranian history, the Shah at times gambled on making concessions—be it the reinstatement of Prime Minister Mohammad Mosaddegh in the 1950s following public revolt—while other times he held firm, like expelling Khomeini in the 1960s. However, the current societal schisms within Iran that were revealed by the 2022-2023 protests may finally be forcing Iran's leadership to contend with a serious, possibly fatal, dictator's dilemma.

The running battles between protesters and police have disappeared from the streets for now, but the "Woman, Life, Freedom" protests still represent a unique and lasting threat to the government. Even if Iran's economy was revived and the myriad government inefficiencies, mismanagement, and corruption were rectified, a critical percentage of the population now see certain freedoms as non-negotiable. To much of the ruling clerical establishment, however, such freedoms are apostasy. Much of Iran's population, for example, opposes strict enforcement of mandatory hijab, which served as the igniting incident of the "Woman, Life, Freedom" protests. More broadly, following Amini's death, large numbers of Iranians took to the streets to fight for certain fundamental rights for women. These demands—some of the most clearly articulated among protesters—represent a radical break from the clerical establishment's worldview of females as second-class citizens who must cover their bodies until they virtually disappear.

For the entire existence of the Islamic Republic, in fact, the Supreme Leader has made repression of women and mandatory hijab fundamental pillars of the revolution. In 2021, well after widespread popular resistance to mandatory hijab was apparent, Khamenei effectively doubled down on this oppression when his hand-picked president initiated a policy of stricter enforcement and punishment. Even if President Pezeshkian were able to somewhat relax some elements of the policing of the Iranian population in the next few years, this marriage between female repression and the modern Iranian state makes it impossible for him to deliver anything resembling the wholesale empowerment of women that large segments of the population support, making compromise or concessions impossible.

Here, then, is a true dictator's dilemma for the Ayatollah. As long as the Islamic Republic fails to grant meaningful rights to women, it will intensify the alienation already felt by many Iranians. For younger Iranians, social media has drawn them to an alternative world in which women aren't arrested for wearing crop-tops or flaunting their hair or singing in public. It just isn't the world where they live. Refusing to grant rights, much less increasing repression, will increase internal contradictions that will continue to, at the very least, materialize into repeated protests. On the other hand, concessions may make the government look both weak to protesters and overly lenient to the very powerful conservative forces in Iran.

Even worse for the regime is the very real possibility that, in repeatedly cracking down on protests for women's rights, Khamenei and the clerical establishment have already mis-stepped. As the widespread repudiation of Iran's theocratic form of government and cynicism about its democratic institutions has made clear, Iranians—particularly younger populations—no longer want to live in the Islamic Republic as it has existed for the past forty-six years. They continue to exist physically in Iran, but, with the help of social media and other digital technology, they have left behind their emotional, spiritual, or intellectual ties to the Islamic Republic.

Brain Drain

Beyond those younger Iranians who have lost faith in the Islamic Republic, the large number of people who have physically fled the country represent a different kind of threat to the authoritarian state: a significant loss of talent for the country. During our interview, Reza Pahlavi, Iran's exiled Crown Prince who now lives in the United States and is well-connected to the country's diaspora, pointed out that "Iranians in the diaspora are involved in industry, in managing companies. They are CEOs. Some of them even run other countries. Imagine the impact that would have for Iran, bringing in the know-how, the knowledge, the connection, the networks and everything."[213]

Iran is not alone in experiencing enormous migratory flow as a result of economic and political misery. Between 2022 and 2023, at least 10 percent of Cuba's population, numbering more than a million people, left the island because they gave up on the possibility of life improving at home and due to a severe economic downturn and harsh government crackdowns on dissent.[214] In a parallel to Iran, Cuba's migration crisis was made worse by the fact that roughly 800,000 of the more than one million Cubans who left the island in recent years were under the age of sixty, representing a significant portion of the country's labor force and economic engine.

Beyond the brain drain that weighs on Iran's economy, expatriates often set up, or contribute financially to various types of, resistance networks outside of Iran. Gazelle Sharmahd was born in Iran two years after the birth of the Islamic Republic. She moved with her family to the West Coast of the United States twenty years ago. By day, Gazelle works as a critical care nurse specializing in coronary care in California. But her main preoccupation is seeking justice for her father's incarceration and subsequent execution.

Her father, Jamshid, was an Iranian-German businessman with American permanent residency. He worked as a software engineer to support his family, oftentimes traveling overseas for work. Seeing Iran devolve into a brutal religious dictatorship, Jamshid began developing an online and radio platform in the early 2000s where he would document the state-sponsored human rights violations being carried out in his homeland. Tehran had already tried silencing him as early as 2009 when he was targeted with death threats. That year, agents hired by the Islamic Republic had attempted to assassinate Jamshid in Los Angeles.²¹⁵ Learning of the assassination attempt at the time, Jamshid said he wasn't surprised to learn from law enforcement officials about the bounty on his head. "Iran is a big power," he said. "There are no rights or laws that they uphold. They're violent against their detractors and this is something every detractor, including myself, knows."²¹⁶ The threats never ceased.

A decade later, in 2020, Jamshid, who by then had been suffering from Parkinson's Disease, was kidnapped by Iranian security forces during a stopover in Dubai en route to India for a business deal involving his software company. Days later, Iranian authorities announced they had captured Sharmahd in a "complex operation" that involved transporting him from Dubai to Oman and, eventually, to Iran, where he was sentenced to death. He was also charged with being the ringleader of the U.S.-based group *Tondar* ("thunder" in Persian) that advocates for the restoration of the pre-1979 monarchy in Iran and was accused of orchestrating a deadly bombing of a mosque in the southern city of Shiraz in 2008 that killed fourteen people, injuring more than 200 others.

Gazelle, Jamshid's daughter, said she supported ceasing all financial support granted to the Islamic Republic by Western governments. The only kind of diplomacy Tehran appreciates, she said, is hostage diplomacy, which it has used dexterously since the embassy hostage crisis of late 1979 to coax out of the U.S. and its allies lucrative financial rewards and prisoner swaps.

"Unfortunately, with American hostages held in Iran, the focus of the U.S. government is more on 'bringing our Americans back home' rather than dealing with the Islamic regime," she said.²¹⁷

As a German citizen and U.S. Green Card holder, Gazelle said that the German and U.S. governments were obligated to work together to jointly secure her father's release, "instead of denying responsibility and playing ping-pong with his life." They failed. "Jimmy would have been able to become a U.S. citizen if he had not been kidnapped and imprisoned. Every single member of his family has done so. Four generations of Sharmahds are now U.S. citizens. What does it say about the Biden administration's moral values when it claims my father is not American enough to stop enduring terror, torture, and execution?"[218]

On Monday, October 28, 2024, after four years in detention, mostly in solitary confinement with no communication with his family, Jamshid was executed. In response, Germany announced it was closing all three of its Iranian consulates in the country, with Germany's Foreign Ministry summoning Iran's chargé d'affaires the next day to protest the execution.

But for Gazelle, who had fought for her father's release every day since his detainment, these actions came too late. Reflecting on her father's unimaginable ordeal, she wrote to me: "Please promise me to not let them get away with this. Promise me to stand strong by our side and demand that the corrupt U.S. and German governments explain why they left my dad to die for four years. Promise me to demand that they investigate what happened and how my dad was killed. Promise me that we demand they bring his body back to us...promise me to continue my dad's path for freedom."[219]

Overcoming Darkness

Another activist, Elahe Tavakolian, is a more recent member of the Iranian diaspora. Days after Mahsa's death on September 21, 2022, she was attending a protest in Esfarayen, located in Iran's northern province of North Khorasan. Thirty-two-years-old at the time, Tavakolian had been at the protest with her ten-year-old twins when she suddenly felt a burning sensation coursing through her head and fell to the ground. "I was soaked in blood and thought I had struck my head on the pavement and broken it when I fell," she later told *Kayhan Life*, an independent news outlet based in London. "A few minutes later, I realized a bullet had hit my eye."[220] Her ten-year-old son kept shouting, "They killed my mother."

Bleeding profusely from her head, taxi drivers were afraid to take Tavakolian to the hospital as it could be interpreted as aiding and abetting dissident activity against the government. Eventually, a civilian couple helped Tavakolian into their car and rushed her to hospital, but nothing could be done to restore her eyesight. Doctors urged her to go abroad for more advanced medical treatment. After sharing her story on Instagram, Tavakolian started getting harassed by Iran's security forces who warned her not to speak out. Her employer in Mashhad, who she claimed had links with the Islamic Revolutionary Guard Corps, fired her.

Tavakolian eventually received sponsorship to get medical treatment abroad, first in Turkey and then in Italy, where she was treated in Milan's San Raffaele Hospital. The bullet was delicately removed from her head. In April 2024, Tavakolian moved to the United States. The "Eyes on Humanity" Fund at Wills Eye Hospital in Philadelphia helped cover the costs of her ophthalmology and surgical treatments and an Iranian plastic surgeon agreed to perform her plastic surgery pro bono. On her GoFundMe page for other medical costs associated with her treatment, she wrote that her treatment plan in the U.S. would include "complex plastic surgery to repair and reposition my right eyelid, release the dense scars, and most likely replace the metallic mesh used for the repair of the fractured right orbital."[221] In a video posted online, Tavakolian revealed her new prosthetic eye.[222]

Tavakolian's blinding was, in fact, part of an organized campaign of terror. Doctors found that at least 580 people lost one or both eyes in Tehran and Kurdistan alone as a result of regime forces firing metal pellets, tear gas canisters, paintball bullets and other projectiles at Iranian protesters.[223] Like many other Iranian women whose eyes were targeted by Iranian security forces, Tavakolian today wears an eyepatch as a defiant reminder of the regime's war on women: she is blinded but refuses to be silenced. Instead, Tavakolian has joined the large diasporic resistance raising awareness of Iran's brutal war on its own people.

On September 26, 2024, Tavakolian addressed the "Iran Conference" hosted by the National Union for Democracy in Iran (NUFDI) in Washington, D.C.[224] Tavakolian, her long hair covering her wounded eye, said, "Mahsa's revolutionary uprising was the largest protest movement against the Islamic Republic." Later in her speech she added:

"For forty-five years we, the people of Iran, have been facing a sect that is against civilization, against Iranian history, against democratic countries, and against the modern world. They have turned Iran into a giant prison and if

anyone disobeys the rules of this prison, it is considered a rebellion, with the most severe consequences. I was shot in the eye because I clenched my fist and shouted, 'Freedom.' My right eye is one of hundreds of eyes that the Islamic Republic deliberately targeted because they, too, cried 'Freedom.' They killed hundreds more and have imprisoned thousands upon thousands to this day—all because they cried out 'Freedom.'...Thousands of young people leave Iran every year to save their futures because the Islamic Republic cannot build a bright future for them...My right eye does not lie. We, the injured of Mahsa's uprising, are living evidence of the Islamic Republic's crimes...We, the people of Iran, have one great hope and that is ourselves. We, the people of Iran, will continue on this path together, relying on our culture and heritage...[and] we will use every opportunity to fight this regime. We, the people of Iran, are writing history. We believe that light will overcome darkness, and soon a day will come that will be remembered forever in history as the victory of the Iranian people."

What Revolution is Next?

President Carter's 1977 comment about Iran being a "sea of stability" in the Middle East was, in a sense, true—just uttered two years prematurely. Since 1979, there have only been two heads of state in Iran, while its neighbors' politics have been much more chaotic. In 1999, Pakistan's government was overthrown in a coup. Eight years later, in 2007, Pakistan's former Prime Minister Benazir Bhutto was assassinated while campaigning. Since 1979, Afghanistan has been invaded by superpowers twice and suffered long stretches of civil war. In 1991, Azerbaijan left the Soviet Union and stumbled through a series of coups in the mid-1990s before arriving at a kind of non-democratic family rule. In 1980 and 1997, Turkey's government was overthrown by military coups, and another one was attempted in 2016. Iraq's Saddam Hussein was overthrown during a 2003 U.S. invasion, after which the country entered into a two-year religious civil war, invasion by ISIS, and general unrest and political conflict. More recently, President Bashar al-Assad's brutal reign in Syria came to an acrimonious ending in December 2024 after his government was overthrown by Syrian rebels, forcing the dictator to flee the country his family had ruled with an iron fist for more than fifty years.

In contrast, the Islamic Republic of Iran has been extremely successful at consolidating power and fending off populist, or military, revolts through periods of democratic or economic discontent. However, it has also never faced the same constellation of challenges to its authority that it does today from foreign adversaries and within. But, as its population makes clear that the Iranian mode of representative rule is insufficient, the Iranian regime will have to either cede power or face growing disquiet. As talented and young citizens literally and figuratively leave behind the strict theocracy, the regime will either need to align its freedoms—including those of women—with Western standards, or be viewed as even more of a repressive anachronism. And, whatever Iran's political future brings, it will have to contend with the issues central to protesters who took over streets, plazas, and social media chanting "Woman, Life, Freedom."

CHAPTER 9
THE OPPOSITION

"We don't have one leader. The beauty and strength of our movement is that every single one of us here is a leader."[225]
—Golshan, women's rights activist in Iran, 2022

Human rights activist Majid Tavakoli is no stranger to the risks of organizing against the Iranian regime. During the widespread protests over the disputed 2009 presidential election, Tavakoli was arrested twice in one year. First in February and, after a 115-day sentence, again in December 2009. His second arrest led to a sentence of up to eight years in prison, during which time he went on a hunger strike and suffered from an untreated respiratory condition.[226] He was conditionally released in May of 2015. Then, in late September 2022, soon after the Amini protests began, Tavakoli was again arrested—after his family's house was raided—and sentenced to five years in prison after voicing support for a liberal democratic system.[227]

In other words, Tavakoli is persistent and committed, but he has also lost faith in Iranians' ability to effectively organize while being monitored by Iran's authoritarian security state. "I think it is not possible to organize inside Iran," he said in 2023. "Even creating effective political solidarity is impossible. It is not possible to create such movements and organizations without the government's knowledge."[228] If Tavakoli is right, then what is the future of efforts to fundamentally change Iran's government?

An Inside-Outside Game

Certainly, some of the Iranian state's success at limiting the success of popular uprisings over the past five decades has been making sure that leading opposition figures are either killed, imprisoned, exiled, or otherwise threatened into remaining silent. This was also true in 2022-23, during which time there was a distinct absence of viable candidates to rally around. Dozens of influential figures within Iran had already been imprisoned when the Mahsa Amini protests peaked, limiting the prospect of effective political opposition leadership emerging from within Iran.

Among them was Nasrin Sotoudeh, a female human rights lawyer with a long history of political activism, as well as an extensive arrest record. Originally a lawyer working in government-controlled organizations, Sotoudeh began using her legal skills to support women's rights. As her activism expanded, she represented opposition activists following the disputed 2009 presidential election, as well as women arrested for not wearing a hijab.[229]

For her efforts, Sotoudeh was arrested in 2010, sentenced to eleven years in prison, and barred from leaving the country or practicing law for twenty years, although her sentence was later reduced to six.[230] Sotoudeh ultimately left prison along with several other human rights activists in 2013 as part of a public relations effort just a few days before President Rouhani addressed the United Nations.

In 2021, Sotoudeh featured in *Time* magazine's list of the 100 most influential people in the world.[231] As a high-profile human rights lawyer who opposed the mandatory hijab, and as a woman who had repeatedly served time in jail for her activism, Sotoudeh would appear an excellent candidate for protesters to rally around in 2022.

Unfortunately, she was already three years into a minimum twelve-year sentence when the protests started. Sotoudeh's continued activist legal work had kept her in the crosshairs of the repressive state apparatus. In 2018, she was arrested and sentenced to jail for ten years.[232] Unbowed, Sotoudeh went on a hunger strike to demand the release of political prisoners and protest prison conditions amid the spread of the coronavirus, which the government was widely seen as mismanaging.

Another steadfast proponent of human rights, Narges Mohammadi, is a member of the Azeri ethnic minority who first got involved in activism while studying physics in university in the mid-1990s. As a result of her pro-human rights journalism and organizing, she initially faced a modest punishment in the form of a ban from the local mountain climbing club. Since then, she had repeatedly endured much worse punishment.

In 2011, she was arrested and sentenced to eleven years. It wasn't her first arrest, but as a result of poor conditions and physical abuse she endured during this imprisonment she experienced a severe decline in health. Since then, Mohammadi has experienced chronic neurological and lung problems.[233] Nonetheless, she and her husband, Taghi Rahmani, have continued their activism, although he eventually left Iran to live in exile in France with their twin daughters.

In 2021, Mohammadi was arrested for the twelfth time in her life, and held in solitary confinement for the fourth. In 2022, she was sentenced to eleven years in prison. In 2023, she was awarded the Nobel Peace Prize.[234] In short, Mohammadi—a female persecuted activist for human rights and Nobel Laureate—was another strong candidate for protesters to rally around, but one who was likewise imprisoned when the "Woman, Life, Freedom" protests broke out.

Not all of the strong candidates for protesters to look to for leadership were inside prisons when the protests broke out, but many other opposition figures were outside the country. The last female Iranian to win a Nobel Peace Prize before Mohammadi, Shirin Ebadi in 2003, served for years as a lawyer defending political activists, during which time several of her clients were murdered and her human rights organizations were shut down by authorities.[235] In 2009, when Ebadi was abroad, her office and house were ransacked by a pro-regime mob, after which she was advised by friends not to return to Iran. Later that year, her Nobel Prize was seized from a lockbox by the IRGC and her bank accounts frozen.[236]

By 2018, she declared that the Islamic Republic was unreformable, in line with the protesters who would take to the streets four years later chanting "Death to the Dictator." However, by the time of the protests, Ebadi had been living in exile in London for fourteen years. Yet another human rights activist, journalist Shiva Nazar Ahari, was also arrested repeatedly beginning in 2009, had her organization supporting human rights journalists, the Committee of Human Rights Reporters, shut down, and faced threats from the regime.[237] She fled Iran prior to the protests and has lived in exile in Ljubljana, Slovenia since 2018.[238]

For decades, the Iranian regime has kept activists on a revolving door through prisons, threatening them and their families and banning them from practicing their craft—a tactic that has become effective at suppressing leadership figures without executing those with international profiles. These repressive tactics again deployed in 2022 and 2023 were certainly effective enough to stop the Islamic Republic, born out of revolution forty-three years earlier, from falling victim to another popular revolt. Instead, it has endured, shunning outrage from the international community while arresting, maiming, and executing anyone that got in its way or posed a threat at home and, at times, abroad.

The deep causes of the protests that began in 2022—a loss of faith in theocracy and demands for real democracy and freedoms, including women's rights—will continue to haunt Iran's ultra-conservative clerical establishment. But, given the concerns of activists like Tavakoli, is it even possible for a coherent opposition leadership to emerge within Iran? And, more to the point, is strong leadership the missing ingredient for the protesters who want to transform Iran's political and social systems?

The Leadership Paradox

The last successful Iranian revolution, in 1979, began with a series of protests and strikes that eventually paralyzed the country and forced the Shah to leave. However, it was not until the various protesters banded around a single leader that the complete overthrow of the civilian government became practically inevitable.

Demonstrators believed that the return of Ayatollah Khomeini from exile on February 1, 1979, would help stamp out an era of dynastic oppression and opulence, ushering in an era of prosperity, equality, and justice for all Iranians. Just ten days later, the government had fallen and Khomeini began to consolidate power.

In contrast, a single leader never emerged during the 2022-2023 "Woman, Life, Freedom" demonstrations. In fact, many protesters proudly declared that their protests were "leaderless." However, once the protests died down and the government remained relatively unchanged, analysts questioned whether a lack of unifying leadership and clearly articulated political goals were one of the primary reasons that the sustained, widespread, and passionate uprising failed to achieve its ultimate objective of regime change. In the case of the 1979 revolution, it's hard to dispute that Khomeini's role, even from exile, was essential. But whether or not a leaderless revolution could replicate that success is not so cut and dry.

Thirty years after Khomeini's triumphant return to Iran, the 2009 Green Revolution had a sort of hybrid approach to leadership. On one hand, it made use of decentralizing tools like the internet and social media. However, it also featured prominent opposition leaders like Mir Hossein Mousavi and Mehdi Karroubi. Both were well-known and respected leaders. Mousavi had served as Iran's last Prime Minister in the late 1980s while Karroubi was a Shia cleric and former speaker of the *majlis*. However, having identifiable leaders in a ruthless authoritarian state also creates significant vulnerabilities for mass movements.

In 2009, when millions of Iranians marched across the country to protest political repression and electoral fraud, which they claimed cost Mousavi the presidency, their momentum was crushed when security forces arrested Mousavi. Likewise, Karroubi was detained in 2011 and held under house arrest at the orders of Khamenei, until August 2024. To this day, Mousavi still remains under house arrest, despite President Pezeshkian's request in 2024 to release him.[239] Khamenei likely keeps Mousavi on a shorter leash because he sees him as potentially a more dangerous opposition figure.

Whether by design—perhaps to avoid the fate of the 2009 protest leaders—or not, no single leader emerged within Iran during the Mahsa Amini protests, which relied much more heavily on digital platforms. At the start of the protests, young activists did band together to form an ad hoc organizing group to help mobilize protesters across Iran using social media and amid serious internet outages. Weeks after Amini's death, groups like Tehran Youth emerged, calling on local Iranians to gather "in all places where mercenaries and repression forces are not present" to chant "Down with the Dictator."[240] Another group, the United Neighborhood Youth, constituting thirty protest organizations, issued on December 11, 2022, a manifesto in favor of a democratic government in Iran that favors equality, ethnic and political freedoms and religious diversity.[241]

However, much of the organizing throughout the country was conducted spontaneously through social media platforms like Instagram, Telegram and TikTok. Everyone had a role to play this time around. Every Iranian had a voice, which many expressed on the streets of Iran, on blogs, on YouTube or on social media.

There were multiple advantages to these almost leaderless movements. For one, the Amini protests were able to organically explode in scope, attracting Iranians of different ages, religious backgrounds, cultures and social strata. Likewise, in a system of government with a track record of crushing popular spurts of revolt, a leaderless, unorganized grassroots combustion of protest is quite possibly the most difficult kind of resistance to quell since there's no center of power for the Islamic Republic to target. With a leader in place, a ruling authoritarian government could incarcerate, excommunicate or execute that individual in the hopes that it strikes a fatal blow in an anti-government movement's momentum. When demonstrators are decentralized in structure and don't have one or two leaders to rally around, it's harder for incumbent forces to squash dissent. There is no head to cut off or, more literally, no single body to hang from a crane.

While the "Woman, Life, Freedom" protests didn't suffer a collapse like the 2009 Green Movement after the arrest of Mousavi, they suffered from the drawbacks common to leaderless movements. One perceived weakness of the latest waves of anti-government protests in Iran was that those protesting were primarily united by a shared resentment for the clerical establishment, rather than a unified positive vision for the Iran they wanted. A leaderless revolution meant the movement lacked direction or a coherent plan for what a post-Ayatollah Iran would look like. The opposition was united in its desire to hasten the demise of the regime, but was fragmented when it came to offering a viable and sustainable alternative to the Islamic Republic. Without sufficient common ground, there was a concern that the protests would eventually become too decentralized and disorganized and would fizzle out. To some onlookers, a spontaneous uprising can draw huge crowds and excitement, and make headlines around the world, but without the presence of strong, unified leadership, those efforts tend to crumble in the face of forceful government crackdowns.

In fact, one of the most coherent plans for a future Iran advanced during the "Woman, Life, Freedom" protests was articulated by Mousavi, the 2009 Green Revolution leader who, though under house arrest, called for a constitutional referendum and wholesale, fundamental political change.[242] But, generally speaking, there was little to no unanimity on forward-looking questions around whether there would be free and fair elections after the fall of the regime; who would fill the leadership vacuum in the immediate aftermath of the theocracy's demise; what role religion would have in society; what would the system of government look like—a constitutional monarchy, a republic, a representative democracy or something else; or what role the international community would play in this transitional period.

If some sort of identifiable leader is needed to finally overthrow the Iranian political system, where might they come from? For the long-time activist Majid Tavakoli, who is currently serving a five-year sentence for his activism in Evin Prison, that organizing and leadership can only come from one place: outside Iran.

Looking to the Diaspora

There are, in fact, a number of prominent dissident Iranians, committed to regime change. Countries like the United States, Canada, the United Kingdom, Germany, and Israel already had sizable populations of Iranian-born expats who left their homeland over the past several decades in search of a better life. Away from the grip of the Islamic Republic and in the safety of the diaspora, this now-global community represented an opportunity for effective political organizing. Opposition forces outside of Iran had a greater chance of growing since independent or reformist parties and voices were severely repressed inside Iran.

Hamed Esmaeilion was one key voice to emerge in the diaspora. By profession, the Iranian-Canadian worked as a dentist in Aurora, north of Toronto. But he also spearheaded efforts to create massive support for a revolution that brought fundamental change to Iran. "I vividly remember September 16, 2022, the day Mahsa died," he recalled.[243] At the time, he was in Toronto working on a documentary about Flight PS752, the Ukraine International Airlines passenger plane shot down over Tehran by the IRGC on January 8, 2020. 176 people were killed, including Esmaeilion's wife, Parisa Eghbalian, and nine-year-old daughter, Reera Esmaeilion.

After Amini's death, Esmaeilion assembled a team to use social media and coordinate simultaneous rallies across the globe, putting Iranian protesters—and the crimes of the Islamic Republic—in the spotlight. Esmaeilion's efforts paid off, staging a synchronized global rally on October 1, 2022 in more than 160 cities. "The rallies started in New Zealand and Australia, stretching from Toronto and Vancouver, to Ecuador, Japan, South Korea, Italy, Sweden—even some cities I hadn't heard of," said Esmaeilion.

In Toronto alone on that day, where Esmaeilion rallied and spoke, he had expected a turnout of 5,000 people, but 50,000 people of all backgrounds showed up. "To me, a successful rally is one where ordinary people come, not just Iranians, and where older generations come."

Later that month, on October 22, 2022, Esmaeilion helped organize a rally in Berlin that drew 100,000 people, all pledging their solidarity for the plight of Iranians back home. "Berlin was a huge success," he said. "All the trains and planes to Berlin that day were full of Iranians, chanting "Woman, Life, Freedom." Berlin was an Iranian city on that day."[244]

The widespread use of social media in Iran has made it increasingly easy for these expats to communicate directly with millions of Iranians. And, of course, there was even a precedent for the return of an exiled figure to lead a mass movement since Khomeini had spent fourteen years in exile prior to the 1979 Revolution.

For decades, prominent Iranian voices, from exiled royals, to actors, sports stars and human rights activists, have used their individual platforms to censure the clerical government. However, during 2022, the dynamic within diaspora opposition changed, with a prominent group setting aside their differences to band together in an encouraging display of unity.

In January 2023, leading figures in the diaspora published coordinated social media posts calling on the international community to designate the Islamic Revolutionary Guard Corps (IRGC) as a terrorist organization.[245] This included Reza Pahlavi, exiled Crown Prince and son of Mohammad Reza Pahlavi, the last Shah of Iran; Nazanin Boniadi and Golshifteh Farahani, popular actresses and activists; Masih Alinejad, a women's rights activist and journalist; Hamed Esmaeilion, author and former president and spokesperson of The Association of Families of Flight PS752; Abdullah Mohtadi, Secretary General of the left-wing Komala Party of Iranian Kurdistan; and Ali Karimi, one of Iran's most legendary footballers now based in Germany.

Their joint statement read: "For more than four decades, the Islamic Revolutionary Guard Corps has been terrorizing and killing civilians inside and outside Iran. Our request for the international community is clear: put the IRGC on the terrorist list. Security forces who join the Iranian people will be welcomed with open arms."

Mahsa's Charter

The following month, in February 2023, all eyes were on Washington, D.C. as eight leading Iranian dissidents gathered in Georgetown University for a televised forum called, "The Future of the Iranian Democracy Movement," to talk collectively about the longevity of the "Woman, Life, Freedom" movement and to share their united vision for Iran's democratic future. The decentralized, social media-driven Mahsa Amini protests inside Iran had created space and hope for a diverse group of exiled long-time proponents of regime change to promote leadership and a unified vision for a fundamentally different Iran.

"For the first time since the uprisings began, eight of the Iranian democracy movement's prominent diaspora leaders will share the stage to talk about the continued viability of the movement, their common vision for Iran's future, and how democratic change in Iran can change the world," read an announcement previewing the Georgetown event.[246]

The event, hosted by the Georgetown Institute for Women, Peace, and Security, marked a turning point necessary for any successful overthrow of the regime: a united leadership abroad representing the pro-democracy movement in Iran. "The Islamic Republic has survived because of our differences, and we should put our differences aside until we come to the polling booth," Nobel Laureate Shirin Ebadi remarked in a video message at the start of the forum. The televised spectacle of many of the most popular opposition voices in the diaspora uniting to form the "Georgetown Coalition" represented an unprecedented threat to a regime that had for years thrived by sowing discord among its detractors.

Activist and journalist Masih Alinejad mentioned her hope that the opposition could agree on a set of democratic principles that would bind them by year-end. "We must agree on principles based on the declaration of human rights, on eliminating discrimination, and principles that every Iranian can see themselves in, and that depict the end of oppression," she said.

Hamed Esmaeilion, whose wife and daughter were killed aboard the Ukraine International Airlines Flight 752 shot down by the IRGC in January 2020, spoke about how, in the wake of Mahsa Amini's death, Iranians were now more united than ever in seeking freedom and justice, enumerating the "four main demands of the revolution" as freedom, due process, social justice, and environmental justice.[247]

State-run media inside Iran was monitoring the Georgetown forum, too, with numerous outlets dismissing the display of unity by the opposition as a manufactured sham, predicting that it would duly collapse. But the fact that Tehran's media mouthpieces had been avidly watching the Georgetown forum meant the regime attributed some importance, or even threat, to the gathering.

On the day of the Georgetown forum, *Nour News Agency*, an IRGC-linked news outlet, wrote: "Disparate counterrevolutionary groups took part in a joint propaganda forum at Georgetown University in the United States...these individuals have fundamental differences of opinion with each other and have repeatedly criticized [one another] ...but are feigning unity...Following several months of unrest, protests and insurrection, calm has fully returned to the country. The enemy's war against the Iranian nation proved fruitless, and by mobilizing the counterrevolution, the efficacy of which the enemy does not believe in, the enemy is using its last card. The enemy is running out of poisonous arrows with which it has hitherto targeted the national unity of Iranians."248

By March 2023, the diaspora leaders published a joint charter, named the "Mahsa Charter," that laid out the demands of the Iranian people inside Iran and abroad. The only way to build a free and democratic Iran, the charter read, was to expunge the Islamic Republic through "unison, organization and relentless continuity in activism." But first the leaders behind the charter emphasized that overwhelming international pressure on the Islamic Republic was the first necessary step to bringing about democratic change in Iran. Other objectives mentioned in the charter included consulting "with democratic governments to expel the ambassadors of the Islamic Republic" and to consult "with democratic governments to expel all dependents of the Islamic Republic from their respective countries."249 A secular-democratic system of government, the charter noted, would encourage more political participation, in contrast to the record low turnout in recent presidential and parliamentary elections.

The Mahsa Charter presented after the Georgetown forum promised to replace Iran's corrupt electoral process with one that was more democratic, stating: "All political and official members of the state shall be elected through a free and democratic election process whereby citizens of all beliefs, ethnicities, gender and sexual orientation be afforded dignity and equal rights before the law."250

While no clear decision had been made on who, if anyone, from the Georgetown opposition group would have emerged as the proposed leader of a future, post-Ayatollah Iran, some influential figures had begun to rally around Reza Pahlavi, the son of Iran's last monarch, whose dynasty was overthrown by Ayatollah Khomeini in the 1979 Islamic Revolution. By mid-January 2023, decorated Iranian footballer Ali Karimi, an outspoken critic of the Islamic Republic, announced to his fifteen million followers on Instagram that exiled Crown Prince Reza Pahlavi was his choice of leader to "overthrow the child-killing regime and hold a free referendum for a free and prosperous Iran."[251]

Some Western governments had even begun recognizing the solidarity group as a legitimate vehicle representing the will of the Iranian people, with Reza Pahlavi, Masih Alinejad and Nazanin Boniadi all being invited to take part in the Munich Security Conference in February 2023, widely seen as the world's preeminent forum for debate on challenges to international security. Officials from the Islamic Republic of Iran and Russia were barred from participating. Iranian and Russian officials had not been invited to participate at the Davos World Economic Forum in Switzerland the month prior, either. Sitting onstage opposite former U.S. Senator Robert Menendez, Pahlavi told the Munich Security Conference that the people of Iran were united in their vision for a post-Ayatollah Iran that is freer and more integrated in the international community. "We need to make a transition as fast as possible because the opportunity costs grow every day that goes by—it becomes more and more costly for Iranians and not just for us but the rest of the world," he said.

"What Iran needs is solidarity in the principles that we are fighting for and we hope to have the support of any country. We are speaking to representatives to help them understand that our ask is for countries to be unified with us in the same way you expect us to be unified on our side."

Cracking Up

The diaspora coalition, fashioned as the Alliance for Democracy and Freedom in Iran (ADFI), could have represented a significant thorn in the side of the Islamic Republic, far from the reach of the country's repressive security forces, but cracks began to emerge within weeks of the Georgetown forum convening. What started out as a promising answer to the perennial question of who might lead a post-Ayatollah Iran ended up being a bitter lesson in how fractured the opposition was while collectively working toward the shared goal of hastening the regime's demise. Over the coming months, those cracks widened, further polarizing key voices in the diaspora who were united in seeking the wholesale overthrow of the regime, but differed on how to get there and on what might come afterwards.

For some in the unified opposition, the cult of personality built around Reza Pahlavi, combined with his aggressive followers online, had become problematic, especially as they started to attack other coalition members on social media. Pahlavi's own liberal-democratic politics and stated goal of a future, secular and democratic Iran countered sharply with the rhetoric of some of his entourage.

Meanwhile, another potential leader, Nazanin Boniadi, temporarily deactivated her Twitter account following a barrage of ad hominem attacks directed at her by Pahlavi followers. On April 21, the unified opposition was dealt another major blow when Iranian-Canadian activist and author Hamed Esmaeilion, who organized the huge rallies in Toronto, Berlin, and cities worldwide, announced that, as a result of "pressure from outside, pressed via undemocratic methods," he was leaving the coalition.

"From the beginning, there were problems and obstacles in the way of organizing, designing and implementing practical plans in the solidarity group," Esmaeilion said. "Both I and other friends inside and outside the solidarity coalition tried to prevent a splintering from happening. We were optimistic until the last moment, but it was useless. Futile fights were ignited, in which the blood of those who were killed [in the protests] and the suffering of those who are in pain are overshadowed."[252]

Esmaeilion later told me that one of the major obstacles in the coalition was that, while there was a general appetite for democratic change, the opposition both inside Iran and abroad lacked the tools and mechanisms to bring about such a system of government in a sustainable way. "We wanted democracy overnight," he said, adding that "Iran is ready for democracy but we don't have the right tools to get there yet."[253]

Esmaeilion added that the Georgetown leadership group drew much support worldwide, but there were also anti-government factions within

Iran that remained skeptical. "Already in Iran, we have very strong voices of opposition, including teachers, workers and nurses, but we're scattered," he said. "A lot of people felt like the diaspora opposition wasn't grassroots and came about after five or six individuals came together and tried to be leaders. Other groups, including the worker unions and teacher unions, didn't believe that they could be led from outside the country. They had their own trusted figures who they would rally around. For them, the revolution has to happen inside Iran."[254]

The "Georgetown Coalition" provided momentary solace for Iranians desperate for a brighter future in Iran. But the group failed to follow through on its objective of offering a robust political alternative to the Islamic Republic.

As Nazanin Boniadi reflected in September 2023, "As with any authoritarian system, the Islamic Republic has persisted through a strategy of divide and rule. Ultimately, the opposition proved to be more fractious than the regime. As long as the regime is united, and we are divided, they will remain in power."[255]

According to Gazelle Sharmahd, members of the fragmented opposition in Iran and abroad carry generational trauma, oftentimes complicating attempts to unify coherently. "The left was traumatized after losing loved ones under the last Shah, Mohammad Reza Pahlavi, and his secret police, SAVAK," said Sharmahd, a Los Angeles-based activist, critical care nurse and daughter of Jamshid Sharmahd, an Iranian-German executed by the Islamic Republic in October 2024 after sitting on death row for four years.[256] "They didn't want the Shah. The people who are nostalgic for the Shah and didn't feel oppressed by him are betrayed by the left who helped topple the Shah and bring about the Islamic regime. Minority groups have been burned because they've been systematically oppressed and killed. Even the Persian language to them is the language of the oppressors. The older generation of the diaspora carry a lot of different traumas that have not healed. In one way, they all want the same thing: freedom, democracy and human rights. But when they're fighting with each other, it's because of their traumas. These triggers have prevented different opposition groups from working together. The Islamic regime knows this and has used it for forty-five years against the diaspora. The Islamic regime knows that if we work together, that's the end of the regime."

But Gazelle remains hopeful about the new generation of Iranians in the diaspora, whose contemporaries bravely led the Mahsa Amini protests inside Iran. "These are the children of those who have experienced trauma first-hand," she said. "They know about it but can distance themselves. They can say: 'I don't care about your flag. I care that you're standing by my side and fighting for the people of Iran, for the political prisoners, for the people who are hanged every six hours, for the girls who are in the streets, for the girls who are being poisoned on the streets, for the people of Kurdistan, for the people who cannot afford to buy anything, for the people who have to go on strikes.' We can distance ourselves from these traumas that prevented our parents' generation from sticking together, and that is the strength we have now in the diaspora."

Pushing For Two Tracks
In an interview following the collapse of the efforts to bring together the diaspora opposition, Reza Pahlavi explained that he thought the diaspora had a limited, but important, leadership role to play in any successful overthrow of the Islamic Republic: "Ultimately, regime change has to be homegrown. Our job, as people from outside of Iran looking in, is in the philosophy of empowerment. How can we best help them? Be their voices to the outside world. Represent their asks when we talk to politicians, when we talk to the press, when we talk to universities or the private sector, so they understand what it is that Iranian people want."[257]

For Pahlavi, the protests failed in their attempts to drive out the conservative clerical establishment because "the protest movement was simply not nurtured. People were on the streets under tremendous hardship and repression and intimidation and terror. Kids were being shot in the eyes and executed, left and right. Braving the streets shows a tremendous amount of motivation, courage, and determination."

He advocates a "dual track approach" to helping Iranians meet that goal of both maximum support for the protesters and maximum pressure on the government. Maximum support would involve initiatives like making information more readily accessible as well as financially supporting demonstrations. "For instance, we have Starlink that people are trying to use to circumvent the regime's limits. There are various ways to smuggle material into the country. There are different ways of trying to get money to Iran."[258] For Pahlavi, well-financed and organized protests could actually bring down the government in a relatively short time frame. "The quickest way to put an end to this regime is ultimately orchestrating major labor strikes across the nation that will paralyze the regime, and there's nothing they can do about it. But it needs to be nurtured, sustained, and financed."[259]

The maximum pressure track would include additional and unified pressure from the United States and European countries. Pahlavi was critical of what he described as the Biden administration's "policy of appeasement of the regime." According to Pahlavi, the U.S. has taken a soft approach on sanctions enforcement, which has allowed Iran to export large amounts of oil. Likewise, the European Union has proved unwilling to declare the IRGC a terrorist organization, as the U.S. has. Pahlavi was also sharply critical of the hostage exchange between Iran and the U.S., in which the U.S. agreed, although later reversed the decision, to give Iran access to six billion dollars in frozen funds. "[I]f they get rewarded by taking hostages...don't expect that behavior to become less aggressive. It will, in fact, embolden them."[260]

Finally, Pahlavi considers the single biggest factor in overthrowing the current government to be encouraging defections from the ruling regime. "We're trying to maximize defections by giving the civilian population and the bulk of the military and paramilitary units assurances that there is a place for them post regime."[261] In this, Pahlavi says there are some lessons from the mistakes made in the U.S.-led regime change in Iraq, in which the bureaucracy and army were dismantled, many of whom joined resistance groups. "This is not the same situation in Baghdad where we send everyone home, and half of the military turns out to become ISIS fighters."

Instead, Pahlavi imagined a system like the Nuremberg Trials in which the Nazi leadership was charged with their crimes, but not "every single soldier that fought in the Nazi army during the Second World War."

Division in the Opposition

The Islamic Republic no doubt sowed divisions in the opposition abroad, while ruthlessly shutting down anti-government groups and individuals from spreading inside Iran. But not all blame for the dissolution of the opposition in the diaspora was of the regime's making. What started out as a ray of hope with the "Georgetown Coalition" coalescing in February 2023—featuring high-profile figures including a Nobel Peace Prize winner, human rights activists, movie stars, a legendary football star and the exiled son of the last Shah of Iran—descended into a failed experiment. A failed experiment for a once-touted, perhaps quixotic, "government-in-exile" that agreed about what it resented—the Islamic Republic and the clerics running Iran for the past forty-five years—but appeared unable to present a vision for a future Iran that everyone in the opposition could rally behind.

At the same time, the episode was a lesson in how to mobilize more effectively next time the regime is vulnerable. The Georgetown group fell short of the ultimate goal of regime change, but the group of immensely popular opposition figures did, however briefly, come together and combine their extraordinarily wide and varied platforms to bring attention to the crimes of the Islamic Republic and demand: "Woman, Life, Freedom."

EPILOGUE: WAITING FOR THE REVOLUTION

On November 2, 2024, videos began spreading across social media of a woman outside the busy entrance to Tehran's Islamic Azad University's Science and Research Branch. The video begins with a woman, later identified as thirty-year-old doctoral student Ahoo Daryaei, sitting at the bottom of the building's cement steps wearing nothing but a bra and underwear.[262] She had reportedly stripped in an act of protest after having been harassed for weeks by Basij paramilitary forces and university police for not covering her hair. Witnesses claimed that her hoodie had been torn during an earlier altercation with security officers, after which she removed the rest of her clothes.[263]

When the video starts, Daryaei is arguing with a man in civilian clothes and, briefly, a woman wearing a black *chador*, both appearing to be members of the security team. After they leave, she wanders through the steady stream of students entering and leaving the school before walking down the adjacent street, where she is eventually surrounded by a group of men—reportedly state security forces—and forced into a car. Witnesses reported that Daryaei had been violently forced into the vehicle, her head was smashed against the side of the car, and blood could be seen on the street after the vehicle left.[264] After that, Ahoo Daryaei disappeared.

The university, which receives funding from the government, released an official statement that Daryaei had been taken to a police station, found to have been suffering from a mental disorder, and sent to a psychiatric health facility.[265] Sources closer to Daryaei claimed that she had no record of mental health issues.²⁶⁶ In Iran, protesters are often sent by authorities to psychiatric centers after being diagnosed as unstable, whatever their actual mental state is.

In a sense, the Islamic Republic has treated all women as unstable, lesser versions of men. In mid-November 2024, the Islamic Republic's agency responsible for enforcing the country's strict religious standards—known formally as the Headquarters for Enjoining the Good and Forbidding the Evil—announced the inauguration of a new specialist mental health clinic in Tehran for women who refuse to wear the hijab. Mehri Talebi Darestani, who was charged with running the Clinic for Quitting Hijab Removal, said the center "will be for the scientific and psychological treatment of removing the hijab, specifically for the teenage generation, young adults, and women seeking social and Islamic identity."²⁶⁷

As footage of Daryaei's detainment spread around the world on X, Instagram, and other social media platforms, some biographical details emerged: Daryaei was a mother of two children who had separated from her husband. The international community also responded to the event. Human rights groups including "Amnesty International" and "Human Rights Watch" called for her release. Mai Sato, the U.N. Special Rapporteur on the Islamic Republic of Iran, wrote on X that she would be "monitoring this incident closely, including the authorities' response." Other reports suggested that Daryaei had been taken into custody by intelligence agents and sent to an undisclosed location.²⁶⁸

Some observers compared Daryaei to Mahsa Amini, but their resemblance was only true in the sense that both were cast and celebrated as heroic women. Aside from reportedly wearing her hijab too loosely for the morality police's taste, Amini had done nothing explicitly political when she was forced into their green and white van. In contrast, Daryaei stripped to her underwear in a very public place in the middle of Tehran after she'd already had an angry confrontation with security. Her protest was explicitly, defiantly political. Nonetheless, Daryaei's protest is an interesting window into the legacy of the "Woman, Life, Freedom" movement ignited by Amini's death a little over two years previously.

The Social Media Trap

Online, videos of the protest were widely shared, with many users celebrating Daryaei's actions as a continuation of the protests sparked by Amini's death. Online comments like, "That brave girl is my leader" proliferated.[269] The hashtag #girlofscienceandresearch also began trending. But other reactions to Daryaei's protest were harder to read.

For example, while the actual incident was playing out in front of the university, some students watched Daryaei from a distance, rapt but laughing and holding their phones up. Other passersby took the opposite approach, intently not looking at a woman wandering outside in her underwear as winter approached, something that would garner attention anywhere, much less in a conservative Islamic state. Notably absent was any obvious support for Daryaei, like clapping, cheering, or creating a protective boundary around her. Likewise, no one tried to intervene when she was abducted, which was noted critically by users on X.

It's hard to know exactly what to make of these reactions. Were students scared of the potentially violent state repression that would likely result from supporting her? Or was Daryaei's protest, not simply burning a hijab but stripping to her underwear, a step too far for students to support anywhere, other than the safer confines of social media?

Likewise, while the majority of social media comments supported Daryaei, a large minority questioned the value of her actions. Among them were cynical comments that she was mentally unstable or already dead, coupled with an array of conspiracy theories. Multiple users commented that Daryaei's actions were not symptomatic of a pro-women protest but a conspiracy promoted by, variously, Iran's reformist President Pezeshkian, the conservative mullahs, or the Israeli intelligence agency Mossad. As one user put it: "Either mental illness or Mossad. Nothing heroic."[270] Were these reactions—filming instead of physically engaging or fact-free dissent into conspiracy theories—evidence of the limitations of social media, which both unified and promoted early protests, but can erode and divide collective action?

Public resistance, state oppression

Regardless of the somewhat muddled scene on social media, women have not stopped resisting the hijab laws since the "Woman, Life, Freedom" movement first ignited, even if their displays of protests—wearing looser or no hijab in public—are subtler than Daryaei's. In fact, this form of everyday defiance has become increasingly commonplace throughout Iran. During the summer of 2024, when wearing the legally mandated combination of headscarf, pants, and a long jacket was particularly oppressive thanks to 100-degree weather (roughly thirty-seven degrees Celsius) in Tehran, the number of women wearing loose or no hijab spiked.[271] While there is a very practical purpose of removing a hijab—cooling down—Iranian women still recognize the political nature of revealing their hair. Photos and videos posted to social media show women without a hijab smiling or giving a thumbs up to the camera. Perhaps even more telling, the phenomenon of not wearing a hijab was more common during the summer nights, when it is cooler, but also easier to escape identification.

Women's continued resistance to the mandatory hijab on Iran's streets has also played out in a political contest at the highest levels of the current government. On September 17, 2024, at a presidential press conference, Maryam Shabani, a journalist for *Andishe Pouya* magazine, explained to Pezeshkian the difficulties women faced when they didn't wear strict hijab.[272] Shabani, wearing a scarf that exposed the hair in the front of her head said, "To get here, I took many shortcuts and back alleys to avoid getting stopped by the morality police."[273]

In response, the President, a self-described reformist who has promised to curb the strict enforcement of hijab, laughed and asked, "Are they still bothering you? That wasn't supposed to happen."[274]

After Shabani assured Pezeshkian that the morality police were still very active in Iran, he replied, "The morality police were not supposed to confront [women]. I will follow up so they don't bother [them]."[275]

The conference itself portended the two worlds that Iranian women exist in the post-"Woman, Life, Freedom" era. Female journalists had traditionally been required to adhere to strict hijab rules at presidential press conferences, but, under Pezeshkian, the dress code was relatively relaxed. To get to this hall of power, though, women had to furtively navigate the streets outside, which were still swarming with the morality police.

In making his assurances, Pezeshkian was likewise not speaking on behalf of a unified government. The following day, the head of the Islamic Republic's Supreme Court, Mohammad Jafar Montazeri, contradicted Pezeshkian, calling for action against Shabani. "Yesterday, a woman with improper dress mocked the Morality Police...Values should not be violated."[276] Montazeri's interjection into the debate was not a surprise. In 2022, the outspoken judge had previously weighed in by calling the "bad hijab" issue a "red line" for the Islamic Republic. At a different time, he supported the Khomeinist line that the hijab was critical for Iran to resist the proliferation of Western culture.[277]

In the run-up to the July 2024 presidential elections, Pezeshkian had campaigned against the *Noor* plan, a series of repressive efforts aimed at women that was instituted by his conservative predecessor, Ebrahim Raisi, and described the initiative as "dark."[278] But despite winning the presidency, Pezeshkian has so far not been able to rein in the morality police, who are controlled by the Supreme Leader. According to the latest U.N. fact finding mission, Iranian women "still live in a system that relegates them to second class citizens."[279] Even as women continued to defy the hijab in public years on from the Mahsa Amini protests, stricter enforcement of modesty laws had stepped up, as the violent detaining of Daryaei highlighted two months later.

Making it Official

The day after the press conference, Pezeshkian also found himself facing another test of his ability to prevent the continued roll out of the *Noor* plan. A controversial series of measures known as the "Law on Protecting the Family through the Promotion of Culture of Chastity and Hijab," originally endorsed by then-President Raisi back in September of 2023, had finally been approved by the Guardian Council. The new law consisted of seventy-one articles, including harsher penalties for anti-hijab activism, expanding the authority of the IRGC, police, and judiciary to locate and prosecute violators. The law seemed to have been drafted with the explicit intention of increasing repression in the areas that it had emerged as important to expanding the "Woman, Life, Freedom" protests. It covered all public spaces, including online spaces. Influencers or public figures who endorsed protests also faced harsher penalties, including fines of 5 percent of their total assets and bans on travel and professional activities.[280] The bill also made official the close surveillance of media outlets, educational institutions and business owners, many of whom had already been shut down because their employees were not wearing a hijab.

Though the bill was in direct opposition with Pezeshkian's avowed politics, he had limited options to stop it from passing into law. Under Iran's system of government, the Parliament and Guardian Council create laws. Once the Guardian Council approved it, Pezeshkian had five days to sign off on the Chastity and Hijab bill. Any attempts at obstructing the bill's passage on his part would be largely nugatory.

On December 13, 2024, the harsher veiling legislation came into force, expanding restrictions on women and girls as young as twelve. Failing to wear a hijab in both physical and online spaces, the legislation stated, would result in extended prison sentences of up to fifteen years, flogging or even death sentences. U.N. experts slammed the new laws as an "intensification of State control over women's bodies in Iran and a further assault on women's rights and freedoms...We call upon the Government of Iran to immediately repeal the Hijab and Chastity Law and all other discriminatory legislation that perpetuates gender-based persecution."[281]

At the same time, Iranian singer Parastoo Ahmadi made headlines after live streaming a concert in an old caravanserai in Iran. Unveiled and accompanied by four male musicians, Ahmadi's twenty-seven-minute performance was designed, as she described it, to "imagine this beautiful homeland" in Iran. Ahmadi went on to say, "I am Parastoo, a girl who wants to sing for the people I love. This is a right I could not ignore; singing for the land I love passionately."[282] Ahmadi was subsequently arrested in Mazandaran, in northern Iran, by regime authorities for defying the hijab laws.

Days later, and after Ahmadi was released on a warning, the implementation of the controversial veiling law was put on pause by the Islamic Republic's National Security Council, with President Pezeshkian describing the legislation as "ambiguous and in need of reform."[283]

End Game

Since the street protests died out in 2023, the conservative regime has shown its desire and ability to suppress conflict and hew to the conservative Khomeinist dogma that has dominated Iranian politics and society for more than four decades. In fact, they may have been too effective at doing so. If the regime made any concessions to the massive popular uprising—a carrot-and-stick approach to re-asserting control—the only carrot was allowing Pezeshkian to run, and win, the presidency. However, by not just handicapping the new President in implementing his own reformist agenda, but forcing through his predecessor's agenda on domestic issues, it appears the regime hasn't offered large segments of alienated Iranians anything at all. By disallowing even a hint of reform, the Iranian regime is essentially guaranteeing a repeat of the protests which could have pushed it over the edge.

Azadeh Pourzand, senior fellow at the Center for Middle East & Global Order and an organizer in the 2009 Green Movement, doubts that the government's policy of retrenchment is feasible. "'Woman, Life, Freedom' divided Iran's history into a 'before' and 'after'. I don't think the regime can take it back to before this movement."[284]

The 2022-2023 protests certainly broke something fundamental in the regime's ability to control its immiserated population. For Spanish Ambassador Losada, who was in Iran while the protests played out, it was the regime itself that was in danger of breaking. "In private talks with the intelligence," claims Losada, "they realized that the government could fall."

In the face of what may have been an existential threat, there are many possible responses. Clearly, the conservative elements in the government resorted to the default: doubling down on repression and restrictions on women's rights. In doing so, Losada thinks the clerics have misjudged the situation. "The government took the worst measures possible by executing people. They executed a few well-known figures to send a strong message to the protesters." Today's continued unwillingness to offer compromise is part and parcel of the same strategy. In short, Iran is firmly in the control of Ayatollah Khamenei and his conservative clerics for now, but the nation remains in a structurally untenable situation.

The confluence of events that may finally topple the regime is hard to predict, as is the weakness behind the state's apparently strong, repressive edifice. Losada suggests that the regime was only saved from further weakening by an external event: the Hamas surprise terror attacks on Israel on October 7, 2023, in which over 1,200 Israelis were killed and more than 250 Israelis and foreign nationals were taken as hostages back into Gaza. "October 7th was Iran's saving grace," said Losada. "It was what pulled them back into the fold and out of the spotlight for domestic problems."[285] However, that same conflict has also led to a systematic dismantling of Iran's proxy forces, as well as direct engagement with Israel's powerful, well-equipped military.

While the United States has frequently played a moderating role in Israel's military engagement with Iran, the re-election of Donald Trump may result in a major shift in those policies to a more aggressive stance. According to Reza Pahlavi, the Trump administration's tougher foreign policy between 2016 and 2020 even led to a drop in executions within Iran.[286] Could the real threat of overwhelming military force create openings for even more fundamental change in Iran?

Aside from external dynamics, Iran's political establishment—already under extreme pressure—is as close to fracturing as just about any time during the past forty-six years. A power struggle over the successor to the Supreme Leader could cause collapse, as could a power grab by the IRGC if it sees the Supreme Leader and his inner circle as so discredited that national security is at risk.

Speculation aside, the regime's inflexibility has bolstered levels of anger and cynicism within the country, setting the stage for a revolution. Without major transformations, the next broad anti-regime coalition may sweep away the Islamic Republic as we know it, just as the 1979 movement swept away the Shah, but what might come next remains as elusive as ever.

ENDNOTES

Chapter 1: The Perils of Punctuation

[1] Iran's judiciary alleges activist has ties to Israeli spy agency, *VOA News*, June 8, 2024

[2] Jackie Northam, An Iranian writer is sentenced to 12 years after tweeting a dot at the supreme leader, *NPR*, September 2, 2024

[3] https://x.com/IranIntl_En/status/1832003079392157923

[4] Farnaz Fassihi, Stymied by protests, Iran unleashes its wrath on its youth, *The New York Times*, November 14, 2022

[5] Deborah Amos, 'Nasrin' documentary spotlights life and work of jailed Iranian human rights lawyer, *NPR*, October 30, 2020

[6] Caroline Hawley, Iran's women on Mahsa Amini's death anniversary: 'I wear what I like now,' *BBC*, September 15, 2023

[7] Robert F. Worth, In Iran, raw fury is in the air, *The Atlantic*, October 1, 2022

[8] Karim Sadjadpour, The question is no long whether Iranians will topple the Ayatollah, *The New York Times*, December 12, 2022

[9] Iran executes 853 people in eight-year high amid relentless repression and renewed 'war on drugs,' *Amnesty International*, April 4, 2024

[10] "Don't let them kill us" – Iran's relentless execution crisis since the 2022 uprising, *Amnesty International*, April 4, 2024

[11] Parisa Hafezi, Iran's 'death committee' president unyielding in defence of clerical rule, *Reuters*, January 17, 2023

[12] Nearly one-third of Iranians struggle below poverty line, *Iran International*, March 2, 2024

[13] President Donald Trump said in his remarks on May 8, 2018 that the United States was withdrawing from the nuclear deal signed in 2015 known as the Joint Comprehensive Plan of Action, or JCPOA. Trump said: "In theory, the so-called 'Iran deal' was supposed to protect the United States and our allies from the lunacy of an Iranian nuclear bomb, a weapon that will only endanger the survival of the Iranian regime. In fact, the deal allowed Iran to continue enriching uranium and, over time, reach the brink of nuclear breakout…A constructive deal could easily have been struck at the time [in 2015], but it wasn't. At the heart of the Iran deal was a giant fiction that a murderous regime desired only a peaceful nuclear energy program."

Chapter 2: Mahsa's Moment

[14] Mahsa Amini's father: "Everything they have said and shown is lies," *Center for Human Rights in Iran*, September 20, 2022

[15] Sajjad Khodakarami and Louise Callaghan, Revealed: the real story of Mahsa Amini's death, *The Times*, March 11, 2023

[16] Diako Alavi, Her name was Mahsa Amini; a swimming coach who wanted to become a doctor, *IranWire*, September 12, 2023

[17] Aida Ghajar, Morality Patrol beats a woman into a coma, *IranWire*, September 15, 2022

[18] Aida Ghajar, Morality Patrol beats a woman into a coma, *IranWire*, September 15, 2022

[19] Excerpt from *PBS Frontline* documentary "Inside the Iranian Uprising," directed by Majed Neisi, June 29, 2023

[20] https://x.com/hdagres/status/1571120629923086336?s=20

[21] Protests break out at funeral of Iranian woman who died after morals arrest, *Reuters*, September 17, 2022

[22] Michael Scollon and Fereshteh Ghazi, How Mahsa Amini's death became a rallying call for thousands of Iranians, *Radio Free Europe/Radio Liberty*, September 13, 2023

[23] Protests break out at funeral of Iranian woman who died after morals arrest, *Reuters*, September 17, 2022

[24] Ambassador Angel Losada, interview with author, November 2024

[25] Despite lethal repression, Iran's protests continue, *The Economist*, October 12, 2022

[26] Ambassador Angel Losada, interview with author, November 2024

Chapter 3: Zan, Zendegi, Azadi

[27] Iran forces kill three more civilians in protest rallies in Kurdistan, *Kurdistan Human Rights Network*, September 21, 2022

[28] Seyma Bayram and Diba Mohtasham, Iran's protesters find inspiration in a Kurdish revolutionary slogan, *NPR*, October 27, 2022

[29] Farangis Ghaderi, *Jin, Jiyan, Azadi* and the historical erasure of Kurds, *International Journal of Middle East Studies*, Cambridge University Press, November 2023

[30] Iran: 'Bloody Friday' crackdown this year's deadliest, *Human Rights Watch*, December 22, 2022

31 Based on the July 18, 2019 report for the United Nations Human Rights Council prepared by Javaid Rehman, the former United Nations Special Rapporteur on the situation of human rights in the Islamic Republic of Iran, who wrote about the regime's excessive use of force and extrajudicial killings of Baluchis and Kurds: https://digitallibrary.un.org/record/3823681

32 Nilo Tabrizy, Iran reaches highest number of executions in nearly a decade, *The Washington Post*, April 4, 2024

33 Sunni Kurdish man executed in Iran, *IranWire*, January 23, 2024

34 https://x.com/AmirToumaj/status/1574227169995378693

35 Brenda Shaffer, How Iran's ethnic divisions are fueling the revolt, Foreign Policy, October 19, 2022

36 https://www.instagram.com/p/CizTmZgAsP1/?hl=en

37 Artemis Moshtaghian, Iranian dissident rapper Toomaj Salehi rearrested less than two weeks after release from prison, *CNN*, November 30, 2023

38 https://www.findagrave.com/cemetery/2761740/aychi-cemetery

39 Based on author's interview with Güneş Murat Tezcür, professor of political science at Arizona State University, March 2024

40 Jamie Dettmer, Fear of the regime, is eroding in Iran, *Politico*, November 4, 2022

41 How "woman, life, freedom" became the slogan for women of the world, *ANF Persian*, November 29, 2015

42 Fiachra Gibbons, Golshifteh Farahani: 'Exile from Iran is like death,' *The Guardian*, September 6, 2012

43 Ali Güler, Golshifteh Farahani: "Jin Jiyan Azadi is a hope," *ANF News*, June 7, 2018

44 Adhiraj Parthasarathy, The legend of Persia's Qurrat al-'Ayn Tahirih, who publicly unveiled and inspired a long revolution, *Scroll*, October 10, 2023

45 Arash Azizi, *What Iranians Want: Women, Life,* Freedom, Oneworld, 2024, page 14

46 Roya Hakakian, The flame of feminism is alive in Iran, *Foreign Policy*, March 19, 2019

47 Jonathan C. Randal, sexual politics in Iran, *The Washington Post*, March 11, 1979

48 Oriana Fallaci, An interview with Khomeini, *The New York Times*, October 7, 1979

49 Oriana Fallaci, An interview with Khomeini, *The New York Times*, October 7, 1979

50 Ayatollah Ruhollah Khomeini, *The Little Green Book*: Selected Fatawah And Sayings Of The Ayatollah Mosavi Khomeini, Bantam Books, 1985, page 27

51 Iranian influential women: Farrokhru Parsa (1922-1980), *IranWire*, October 31, 2023

⁵² Nasrin Sotoudeh, *Women, Life, Freedom: Our Fight for Human Rights and Equality in Iran*, Cornell University Press, 2023, page 17

⁵³ https://www.theglobaleconomy.com/Iran/Female_literacy_rate_15_25/

⁵⁴ Fariba Parsa, Temporary marriage in Iran and women's rights, *Middle East Institute*, January 13, 2021

⁵⁵ Maryam Banihashemi, interview with author, February 2024

⁵⁶ Sussan Tahmasebi, The One Million Signatures Campaign: an effort born on the streets, *International Civil Society Action Network*, September 14, 2013

⁵⁷ Nassim Hatam, Why Iranian women are wearing white on Wednesdays, *BBC*, June 13, 2017

⁵⁸ https://x.com/JonathanHaroun1/status/1645821406192586757

⁵⁹ Iranian morality police fire warning shots after crowd prevents arrest of women without hijab, *The Telegraph*, February 19, 2019

⁶⁰ Iran's leader ordered crackdown on unrest – 'Do whatever it takes to end it,' *Reuters*, December 23, 2019

⁶¹ Vivian Yee and Farnaz Fassihi, Women take center stage in antigovernment protests shaking Iran, *The New York Times*, September 26, 2022

⁶² Belgian foreign minister cuts hair in parliament in support of Iranian women, *Reuters*, October 7, 2022

⁶³ Darya Safai, interview with author, August 2023

⁶⁴ Maya Oppenheim, 'Act of cowardice': Mural of Marge Simpson chopping off hair in solidarity with Iran protests removed, *Independent*, October 7, 2022

Chapter 4: A Culture of Protest: From Crown to Turban

⁶⁵ Mehrnoush Cheragh Abadi, Remembering Mossadegh: the anti-imperialist icon that Tehran, London and Washington would rather forget, *Equal Times*, March 16, 2020

⁶⁶ Andrew Scott Cooper, *The Fall of Heaven: The Pahlavis and the Final Days of Imperial Iran*, Henry Holt and Co., 2016, page 163

⁶⁷ Andrew Scott Cooper, *The Fall of Heaven: The Pahlavis and the Final Days of Imperial Iran*, Henry Holt and Co., 2016, page 163

⁶⁸ Abdar Rahman Koya (editor), *Imam Khomeini: Life, Thought and Legacy*, Islamic Book Trust & Crescent International, 2009, page 150

⁶⁹ Cheryl Bernard and Zalmay Khalilzad, *"The Government of God:" Iran's Islamic Republic*, Columbia University Press, 1984, page 110

⁷⁰ Mathias Braschler and Monika Fischer, The women forced out of Iran: 'Every act of resistance is a spark of hope,' *The Guardian*, March 18, 2023

⁷¹ R. W. Apple Jr., Khomeini arrives in Teheran, urges ouster of foreigners; millions rally to greet him, *The New York Times*, February 1, 1979

⁷² Report: Ayatollah Ali Khamenei: Supreme Leader of the Islamic Republic of Iran, *United Against Nuclear Iran*, August 2023

⁷³ Liz Thurgood, Bakhtiar quits after losing army backing, *The Guardian*, March 12, 1979

⁷⁴ One person's story: Shapur Bakhtiar, *Abdorrahman Boroumand Center for Human Rights in Iran*, https://www.iranrights.org/memorial/story/-8733/shapur-bakhtiar

⁷⁵ Ronald Koven, Effort to kill Iranian exile fails in Paris, *The Washington Post*, July 19, 1980

⁷⁶ John Irish and Michaela Cabrera, Iran's first president says Khomeini betrayed 1979 Islamic revolution, *Reuters*, February 4, 2019

⁷⁷ Arash Azizi, Is Iran a country or a cause, *The Atlantic*, May 1, 2024

⁷⁸ Michael Axworthy, *Revolutionary Iran: A History of the Islamic Republic*, Oxford University Press, 2013, page 401

⁷⁹ The Green Movement's name can be traced back to when Mohammad Khatami, Iran's reformist, two-term president, gave a green sash to Mir Hossein Mousavi.

⁸⁰ Ian Black and Saeed Kamali Dehghan, Riots erupt in Tehran over 'stolen' election, *The Guardian*, June 13, 2009

⁸¹ Michelle English, Q&A: Pouya Alimagham on the protest movement in Iran, *MIT News*, December 6, 2022

⁸² Ian Black and Saeed Kamali Dehghan, Riots erupt in Tehran over 'stolen' election, *The Guardian*, June 13, 2009

⁸³ Saeed Kamali Dehghan and Matthew Taylor, Neda Agha Soltan: 'She is dead but regime is still afraid of her,' *The Guardian*, June 11, 2010

⁸⁴ Iranian says militiaman killed protester, *Associated Press*, June 25, 2009

⁸⁵ Saeed Kamali Dehghan, Neda Soltan's family 'forced out of home' by Iranian authorities, *The Guardian*, June 24, 2009

⁸⁶ Ian Black, Film about Iranian protest victim Neda Agha-Soltan beats regime's censors, *The Guardian*, June 4, 2010

87 Nazila Fathi, In a death seen around the world, a symbol of Iranian protests, *The New York Times,* June 22, 2009

88 Hooman Majd, Think again: Iran's Green Movement, *Foreign Policy,* January 6, 2010

89 Shortly after its creation in 1979, the Islamic Republic announced a mandatory Islamic dress code, as well as rollbacks in family law rights and the establishment of the morality police to enforce these laws on the streets of Iran. Tens of thousands of women in Iran protested against these restrictive laws in Tehran in 1979, but their protestations fell largely on deaf ears as the then-nascent theocratic elites continued to consolidate power and enforce these socio-cultural policies.

90 Ellen Ioanes, Iran's months-long protest movement, explained, *Vox,* January 15, 2023

91 As Iran scares the Middle East, at home its regime rots, *The Economist,* February 28, 2024

92 Iran: Two years after 'Woman Life Freedom' uprising, impunity for crimes reigns supreme, *Amnesty International,* September 11, 2024

93 Parham Ghobadi, Iranian woman paralysed after being shot over hijab, *BBC,* August 12, 2024

Chapter 5: Social Media in Iran

94 Video of woman unveiling at Tehran engineers event goes viral, *Iran International,* February 17, 2023

95 Holly Dagres, Iranians on #socialmedia, *The Atlantic Council,* January 2022

96 Babak Dehghanpisheh, The killing of a 9-year-old boy further ignites Iran's anti-government protests, *The Washington Post,* November 18, 2022

97 Babak Dehghanpisheh, The killing of a 9-year-old boy further ignites Iran's anti-government protests, *The Washington Post,* November 18, 2022

98 Young man shot dead as Iranian authorities try to silence justice-seeking families, *Center for Human Rights in Iran,* June 12, 2023

99 Internet disrupted in Iran amid protests over death of Mahsa Amini, *NetBlocks,* September 19, 2022

100 Hardliner regime insider calls for execution of VPN retailers, *Iran International,* February 8, 2023

101 Freedom House slams Iran for censoring online election criticism, *Iran International,* October 17, 2024

102 Editorial board, How the battle democracy will be fought – and won, *The Washington Post,* December 21, 2023

103 Reza Pahlavi, interview with author, February 2024

¹⁰⁴ Noushin Ahmadi Khorasani, Why the "Girls of Revolution Street" movement did not spread, *Radio Zamaneh*, December 18, 2018

¹⁰⁵ Dominic Yeatman, Iranian mother kills herself after security forces 'beat daughter to death', *Metro*, October 10, 2022

¹⁰⁶ Mass poisoning of schoolgirls in Iran, *The Iran Primer*, April 4, 2023

¹⁰⁷ Parisa Hafezi, Iran's Khamenei calls girls' poisoning 'unforgivable' after public anger, *Reuters*, March 7, 2023

¹⁰⁸ https://x.com/Hozier/status/1578479749050925056

¹⁰⁹ Bart Lenaerts-Bergmans, What is spear-phishing? Definition with examples, *Crowdstrike*, November 5, 2023

¹¹⁰ https://x.com/RKOTOfficial/status/1628006409651605504

¹¹¹ https://x.com/certfalab/status/1629083372570959872

¹¹² AJ Vicens, Iran-linked hackers used fake Atlantic Council-affiliated persona to target human rights researchers, *CyberScoop*, March 9, 2023

¹¹³ Patrick Wintour, 'It is not possible to organise in Iran': jailed activist warns of totalitarianism after Mahsa Amini protests, *The Guardian*, September 15, 2023

¹¹⁴ Video: controversial gathering of teenagers in Shiraz; several people arrested, *Fararu*, June 24, 2022

¹¹⁵ Gianluca Mezzofiore, Katie Polglase and Adam Pourahmadi, What really happened to Nika Shahkarami? Witnesses to her final hours cast doubt on Iran's story, *CNN*, October 27, 2022

¹¹⁶ Gianluca Mezzofiore, Katie Polglase and Adam Pourahmadi, What really happened to Nika Shahkarami? Witnesses to her final hours cast doubt on Iran's story, *CNN*, October 27, 2022

¹¹⁷ https://www.instagram.com/p/C2LOiTjOLAr/?utm_source=ig_web_copy_link&igsh=MzRlODBiNWFlZA==

¹¹⁸ Akhtar Safi and Solmaz Eikdar, Mother of slain protester denounces state TV whitewash, *IranWire*, October 6, 2022

¹¹⁹ Excerpt from *PBS Frontline* documentary "Inside the Iranian Uprising," directed by Majed Neisi, June 29, 2023

¹²⁰ Megan Harwood-Baynes, 'We want everyone to know her name': TikToker Hadis Najafi, 23, shot dead in Iran protests, *Sky News*, September 30, 2022

¹²¹ https://x.com/IranNW/status/1574017864876511232

Chapter 6: Creative Resistance in Music, Art and Dance

148   UNVEILED

[122] "A song can unite, inspire and ultimately change the world," Dr. Jill Biden said at the Grammys. "[*Baraye is*] a powerful and poetic call for freedom and women's rights…Shervin may have been arrested but this song continues to resonate around the world with its powerful theme: Woman, Life, Freedom."

[123] https://www.youtube.com/watch?v=oIERTHlsPOU

[124] https://time.com/collection/100-most-influential-people-2023/6269445/shervin-hajipour/

[125] In 2013, the World Health Organization included four Iranian cities in its list of the ten most polluted cities in the world.

[126] Watch Holly Dagres' TEDx talk, "How Iran's Gen Z imagines a better, different future," September 4, 2024: https://www.youtube.com/watch?v=XtUotLlcYlw

[127] Pirouz ("Victory") was a rare Persian cheetah that had captured the hearts and minds of millions of Iranians worldwide. During the "Woman, Life, Freedom" protests, Pirouz, five-months-old at the time, had become a symbol of national pride and hope to people fighting for a freer Iran. Pirouz's death from kidney failure in late February 2023 sparked outrage among Iranians who blamed the government's woeful disregard for the country's environment and its endangered species. "In the shadow of the Islamic Republic, neither animals nor humans are safe," tweeted Iranian football coach and former national player Ali Karimi shortly after Pirouz's death.

[128] https://www.youtube.com/watch?v=mIkKozqJWvw

[129] The opening lyrics of Shervin Hajipour's hit song mentions dancing for freedom: "For dancing in the alleys."

[130] Clarissa-Jan Lim, Iranian women are re-creating a viral TikTok dance without hijabs on after 5 teens who did the same were reportedly detained and forced to make an apology video, *BuzzFeed News*, March 17, 2023

[131] Singer Selena Gomez expresses support for Iranian dancing girls, *Iran International*, March 18, 2023

[132] https://www.instagram.com/p/Cpj460_LxKM/?hl=en

[133] Cora Engelbrecht, A couple danced in Tehran's streets. Now they are in prison, *The New York Times*, February 1, 2023

[134] https://x.com/AlinejadMasih/status/1619973932223983617

[135] Aina J. Khan, Iran imprisons couple shown dancing at Tehran's Freedom Tower in viral video, *NBC News*, February 1, 2023

[136] https://www.instagram.com/zhatiis/?igshid=YmMyMTA2M2Y%3D

[137] https://www.instagram.com/p/Cy8asHXIbPU/

138 https://twitter.com/amirreiis/status/1749073273047204335

139 Christina Lamb, The world's bravest rapper – could you match his courage, *The Times,* October 22, 2023

140 The opening lines of Toomaj Salehi's *Rat Hole* track released on July 28, 2021: https://www.youtube.com/watch?v=k0XMnGrDy-w&t=19s

141 Protesting rapper's video foretelling Iranian regime's future leads to arrest as fans fear for his life, *Radio Free Europe/Radio Liberty,* November 8, 2022

142 Iranian dissident rapper Toomaj Salehi released from prison, *Iran International,* December 1, 2024

143 Niamh Kennedy and Artemis Moshtaghian, Iranian dissident rapper Toomaj Salehi cleared of charge after death sentence overturned, *CNN,* August 14, 2024

144 David Gritten, Mohsen Shekari: Iran carries out first execution over protests, *BBC,* December 8, 2022

145 Erin Argun, Art as activism: how protest art challenges the status quo, *My Art Broker,* August 30, 2024

146 Mathias Braschler and Monika Fischer, The women forced out of Iran: 'Every act of resistance is a spark of hope,' *The Guardian,* March 18, 2023

147 https://www.whitehouse.gov/briefing-room/statements-releases/2022/11/02/statement-by-vice-president-kamala-harris-on-iran-protests-and-the-un-commission-on-the-status-of-women/

148 Will Heinrich, With 'Eyes on Iran,' artists bring protests to Roosevelt Island, *The New York Times,* December 8, 2022

149 Eyes on Iran art activation faces the U.N. in New York, *GlobeNewswire press release,* November 28, 2022

150 Michelle Nichols, Iran ousted from U.N. women's group after U.S. campaign, *Reuters,* December 14, 2022

Chapter 7: The Duel in Doha

151 Maryam Sinaiee, Iran's regime grapples with female athletes and hijab dilemma, *Iran International,* August 29, 2023

152 https://x.com/danroan/status/1594630560244178946?s=20

153 https://x.com/iranintlsport/status/1592441519331774465

154 Robert Tait, Fifa suspends Iran for 'government meddling,' *The Guardian,* November 24, 2006

155 Iran arrests outspoken player Voria Ghafouri amid World Cup scrutiny, *Associated Press*, November 24, 2022

156 Sardar Pashaei, interview with author, August 2023

157 Jonathan Harounoff, Political football: U.S. and Iran prepare for historic World Cup match, *Haaretz*, July 20, 2022

158 Trump calls on Iran not to execute wrestling star Navid Afkari, *Reuters*, September 3, 2020

159 Maryam Afshang, Iran protests: 15 minutes to defend yourself against the death penalty, *BBC*, January 18, 2023

160 Maryam Afshang, Iran protests: 15 minutes to defend yourself against the death penalty, *BBC*, January 18, 2023

161 Shiva Amini, interview with author, July 2022

162 Mathias Braschler and Monika Fischer, The women forced out of Iran: 'Every act of resistance is a spark of hope,' *The Guardian*, March 18, 2023

163 https://x.com/KosovareAsllani/status/1171383260036964354

164 https://x.com/IranIntl_En/status/1582851603672887296

165 John Duerden, Iranian women allowed into football stadiums but journey is far from over, *The Guardian*, January 25, 2024

166 Colin Millar, Iran, women and the ongoing struggle for football 'freedom,' *The Athletic*, July 29, 2024

167 Mathias Braschler and Monika Fischer, The women forced out of Iran: 'Every act of resistance is a spark of hope,' *The Guardian*, March 18, 2023

168 Sarah Sfeir, From Iran to France, how Sadaf Khadem became a boxer and champion of women's rights, *Arab News*, October 17, 2022

169 Sarah Sfeir, From Iran to France, how Sadaf Khadem became a boxer and champion of women's rights, *Arab News*, October 17, 2022

170 Kevin Baxter, Iran World Cup showdown with U.S. overshadowed by protests against Islamic regime, *Los Angeles Times*, November 28, 2022

171 Sam Kiley, Iran threatened families of national soccer team, according to security source, *CNN*, November 29, 2022

172 Woman wearing Mahsa Amini top stopped at World Cup game, *BBC*, November 25, 2022

[173] Qatari police confront female fan wearing 'Woman, Life, Freedom' t-shirt at Iran match, *Storyful,* November 25, 2022

[174] David Gritten, World Cup 2022: man killed in Iran celebrating football team's loss, *BBC,* November 30, 2022

[175] Payam Younesipour, The disastrous impact of ideology on Iranian chess, *IranWire,* July 25, 2023

Chapter 8: A Dictator's Dilemma

[176] Excerpt of Ayatollah Khomeini's 1980 speech found on the Middle East Research and Information Project's website: https://merip.org/1980/06/khomeini-we-shall-confront-the-world-with-our-ideology/

[177] Ebrahim Raisi: What we know about deadly Iran helicopter crash, *BBC,* May 20, 2024

[178] Ebrahim Raisi: What we know about deadly Iran helicopter crash, *BBC,* May 20, 2024

[179] Sanya Burgess, Inside Iran's silent resistance movement defiantly celebrating president's death, *The i Paper,* May 22, 2024

[180] Deepa Parent, 'People are in no mood to mourn': mixed reactions in Tehran after death of President Ebrahim Raisi, *The Guardian,* May 20, 2024

[181] Erika Solomon and Farnaz Fassihi, Ebrahim Raisi, Iran's president, dies in helicopter crash at 63, *The New York Times,* May 20, 2024

[182] Erika Solomon and Farnaz Fassihi, Ebrahim Raisi, Iran's president, dies in helicopter crash at 63, *The New York Times,* May 20, 2024

[183] George Hay and Yawen Chen, President's death makes Iran even less predictable, *Reuters,* May 20, 2024

[184] https://telewebion.com/episode/0xd37244e

[185] Treasury targets billion dollar foundations controlled by Iran's supreme leader, *U.S. Department of the Treasury press release,* January 13, 2021

[186] Ambassador Angel Losada, interview with author, November 2024

[187] Saeid Golkar and Kasra Aarabi, Iran's election circus has just begun, *War on the Rocks,* June 17, 2024

[188] Sanam Vakil: Iran's trajectory after Raisi, *Center for Strategic & International Studies (CSIS),* May 29, 2024

[189] Marie Abdi, Moving to a post-Khamenei era: cutthroat competition within the supreme leader's office, *Middle East Institute,* February 29, 2024

190 Marjan Keypour, As the threat of conflict grows, Khamenei's son is back in the spotlight, *The Atlantic Council,* October 10, 2024

191 Marjan Keypour, As the threat of conflict grows, Khamenei's son is back in the spotlight, *The Atlantic Council,* October 10, 2024

192 Potkin Azarmehr, Khamenei's son suspends his religious lectures, *The American Spectator,* September 27, 2024

193 Morad Veisi, Who are Khamenei's likely successors?, *Iran International,* November 17, 2024

194 Will Rouhani help decide Iran's next supreme leader, *Amwaj Media,* November 27, 2023

195 Marie Abdi, Moving to a post-Khamenei era: cutthroat competition within the supreme leader's office, *Middle East Institute,* February 29, 2024

196 Ali Alfoneh, Khamenei's succession dilemma: to name or not to name a successor-designate?, *The Arab Gulf States Institute in Washington,* December 7, 2023

197 Iranian official close to leader issues rare warning over crackdown, *Radio Free Europe/Radio Liberty,* December 12, 2022

198 Iranian official close to leader issues rare warning over crackdown, *Radio Free Europe/Radio Liberty,* December 12, 2022

199 Iranian official close to leader issues rare warning over crackdown, *Radio Free Europe/Radio Liberty,* December 12, 2022

200 David Gritten and Sam Hancock, Majidreza Rahnavard: Iran carries out second execution over protests, *BBC,* December 12, 2022

201 Armin Rosen, Americans love America like Iranian rebels do, *AlArabiya News,* December 30, 2022

202 Ambassador Angel Losada, interview with author, November 2024

203 David Gritten and Sam Hancock, Majidreza Rahnavard: Iran carries out second execution over protests, *BBC,* December 12, 2022

204 Rate of voter turnout for presidential elections in the Islamic Republic of Iran from 1980 to 2024, *Statista,* July 2024

205 Iran begins first election campaign since 2022 mass protests, *Associated Press,* February 22, 2024

206 As Iran scares the Middle East, at home its regime rots, *The Economist,* February 28, 2024

207 Vivian Yee, Iranian hard-liner Ebrahim Raisi wins presidential vote, *The New York Times,* June 19, 2021

208 Patrick Wintour, Iran election: turnout sinks to record low as polls close, *The Guardian,* March 1, 2024

209 Iran at the crossroads: have the mullahs lost their grip, *The Week*, March 16, 2024

210 Ex-Iranian president Khatami hails reformism after voting abstention, *IranWire*, March 6, 2024

211 Saeed Azimi, Iran elections: record-low turnout shows even regime loyalists are unhappy, *The Stimson Center*, July 1, 2024

212 Karim Sadjadpour, The question is no long whether Iranians will topple the Ayatollah, *The New York Times*, December 12, 2022

213 Reza Pahlavi, interview with author, February 2024

214 Nora Gámez Torres, Cuba admits to massive emigration wave: a million people left in two years amid crisis, *Miami Herald*, July 24, 2024

215 Man who targeted Iran critics skips LA court date, *Associated Press*, December 3, 2010

216 Man who targeted Iran critics skips LA court date, *Associated Press*, December 3, 2010

217 Gazelle Sharmahd, interview with author, August 2023

218 Gazelle Sharmahd, Bring my father Jamshid Sharmahd back from Iran, *The New York Post*, September 2, 2023

219 Gazelle Sharmahd, interview with author, October 2024

220 Ahmad Rafat, Elahe Tavakolian, who lost eyesight in Iran protests, bears witness, *Kayhan Life*, April 21, 2023

221 https://www.gofundme.com/f/please-help-elaheh-tavakoliyans-treatment

222 https://x.com/sarahraviani/status/1659222814954602496

223 Aida Ghajar and Roghayeh Rezaei, Blinding as a weapon: The face with a white heart, *IranWire*, February 20, 2023

224 https://www.youtube.com/watch?v=gamV2YyyyqY&t=14s

Chapter 9: The Opposition

225 Quotation of the day: Iranians' long-held rage adds fuel to protests, *The New York Times*, September 27, 2022

226 Jailed student activist breaks his hunger strike, *Radio Free Europe/Radio Liberty*, May 30, 2010

227 Iranian activist Tavakoli starts five-year prison sentence, *Radio Free Europe/Radio Liberty*, October 7, 2023

228 Patrick Wintour, 'It is not possible to organise in Iran': jailed activist warns of totalitarianism after Mahsa Amini protests, *The Guardian*, September 15, 2023

229 Jeannette Catsoulis, 'Nasrin' review: righting wrongs in Iran, *The New York Times*, December 17, 2020

230 Saeed Kamali Dehghan, Iranian lawyer Nasrin Sotoudeh has jail sentence reduced, *The Guardian*, September 14, 2011

231 Iranian activist Sotoudeh receives prestigious German award, *Iran International*, November 14, 2023

232 Iran: Arrest of prominent human rights lawyer Nasrin Sotoudeh is an outrage, *Amnesty International*, June 13, 2018

233 Iranian Peace laureate Mohammadi: 'lioness' locked up for challenging Tehran, *Reuters*, October 6, 2023

234 Diba Mohtasham, Children of jailed Iranian activist Narges Mohammadi accept her Nobel Peace Prize, *NPR*, December 11, 2023

235 Shirin Ebadi's profile found in Britannica.com: https://www.britannica.com/biography/Shirin-Ebadi

236 Shirin Ebadi Nobel Peace Prize medal 'seized by Iran,' *BBC*, November 27, 2009

237 Iran urged to drop prison sentences against human rights activists, *Amnesty International*, January 10, 2011

238 Aida Ghajar, Shiva Nazar Ahari: solitary confinement and quarantine both isolate you from society, *IranWire*, April 1, 2020

239 Iran's president negotiates release of opposition leader Mehdi Karroubi, *Middle East Eye*, August 28, 2024

240 Maryam Sinaiee, Underground youth group in Iran emerging as protest leader, *Iran International*, October 14, 2022

241 Nicholas Carol and Frederick W. Kagan, Iran crisis update, *Institute for the Study of War*, December 11, 2022

242 Mir Hossein Mousavi dismissed from head role of Iran's Academy of Arts, *Radio Farda*, December 23, 2009

243 Hamed Esmaeilion, interview with author, November 2024

244 Hamed Esmaeilion, interview with author, November 2024

245 https://x.com/hdagres/status/1614729731726770177?s=20

246 https://www.instagram.com/georgetown_wps/p/CoXwCQcJxfu/

247 Prominent Iranian dissidents unite to discuss democracy movement, *VOA News*, February 11, 2023

248 Ali Alfoneh, The Islamic Republic reacts to opposition forum at Georgetown University, *The Arab Gulf States Institute in Washington*, February 14, 2023

249 Jonathan Harounoff, Iran's opposition has no idea who or what should come next, *The Jewish Chronicle*, August 31, 2023

250 The charter of solidarity and alliance for freedom (the Mahsa Amini charter), March 9, 2023: https://giwps.georgetown.edu/wp-content/uploads/2023/02/MahsaCharterEnglish-82d794a467804573844b82161bc604b2.pdf

251 https://x.com/JonathanHaroun1/status/1615520747350269955?s=20

252 https://x.com/esmaeilion/status/1649513329969229827?s=20

253 Hamed Esmaeilion, interview with author, November 2024

254 Hamed Esmaeilion, interview with author, November 2024

255 Nazanin Boniadi, The 44-year riddle of Iran's democratic opposition, *IranWire*, September 5, 2023

256 Gazelle Sharmahd, interview with author, August 2023

257 Reza Pahlavi, interview with author, February 2024

258 Reza Pahlavi, interview with author, February 2024

259 Reza Pahlavi, interview with author, February 2024

260 Reza Pahlavi, interview with author, February 2024

261 Reza Pahlavi, interview with author, February 2024

Epilogue: Waiting for the Revolution

262 Akhtar Makoii, Iran student strips in protest over strict hijab dress code, *The Telegraph*, November 3, 2024

263 Akhtar Makoii, Iran student strips in protest over strict hijab dress code, *The Telegraph*, November 3, 2024

264 https://www.instagram.com/p/DB3l-4yI2B-/

265 Jacqueline Howard, Iran says woman detained after undressing released without charge, *BBC*, November 19, 2024

266 Amnesty demands releasee of Ahoo Daryaei, who was 'violently arrested' after stripping off to protest strict Islamic dress code, reports say, *Sky News,* November 4, 2024

267 Melanie Swan, Iran sets up mental health clinic to 'treat' women who refuse to wear hijab, *The Telegraph,* November 13, 2024

268 Where is Ahoo Daryaei, Iranian woman arrested after stripping at university, *Firstpost,* November 4, 2024

269 Akhtar Makoii, Iran student strips in protest over strict hijab dress code, *The Telegraph,* November 3, 2024

270 https://x.com/khansarinia/status/1852709954081202543

271 Jon Gambrell, Women in Iran going without hijabs as the 2nd anniversary of Mahsa Amini's death approaches, *Associated Press,* September 14, 2024

272 Frances Mao, Iran's morality police will not 'bother' women, president says, *BBC,* September 16, 2024

273 Solmaz Eikdar, Mandatory hijab sparks first clash between Pezeshkian and judiciary, *IranWire,* September 18, 2024

274 Solmaz Eikdar, Mandatory hijab sparks first clash between Pezeshkian and judiciary, *IranWire,* September 18, 2024

275 Frances Mao, Iran's morality police will not 'bother' women, president says, *BBC,* September 16, 2024

276 Solmaz Eikdar, Mandatory hijab sparks first clash between Pezeshkian and judiciary, *IranWire,* September 18, 2024

277 Solmaz Eikdar, Mandatory hijab sparks first clash between Pezeshkian and judiciary, *IranWire,* September 18, 2024

278 Maryam Dehkordi, 100 days in: Pezeshkian's policies deepen concerns for women's rights, *IranWire,* November 5, 2024

279 Frances Mao, Iran's morality police will not 'bother' women, president says, *BBC,* September 16, 2024

280 Iran: New hijab law adds restrictions and punishments, *Human Rights Watch,* October 14, 2022

281 Iran: UN experts call for strict new hijab law to be repealed, *UN News,* December 14, 2024

282 Doha Madani, Singer in Iran arrested after performing on YouTube without a hijab, *NBC News,* December 15, 2024

283 Jiyar Gol, Iran pauses controversial new dress code law, *BBC,* December 16, 2024

[284] Leela Jacinto, Iran's regime has crushed anti-veil protests, but it has 'lost the battle' for credibility, *France 24*, September 12, 2023

[285] Ambassador Angel Losada, interview with author, November 2024

[286] Reza Pahlavi, interview with author, February 2024

ACKNOWLEDGEMENTS

This book would not have come to fruition without the instrumental help of my loving family, friends, colleagues, and editors. I am eternally grateful to the many extraordinary people around me, without whom my life wouldn't be what—and where—it is. Without them, this book would have remained a mere abstraction.

A special thank you to:

- Stephanie, my loving wife, for being the greatest partner in life, best friend and book editor that one could ask for. Meeting you on the steps of Q staircase at Jesus College on my first day as a Cambridge undergraduate remains the best day of my life. Every day I'm inspired by your achievements, both personal and professional. Without you, this book would never have materialized and I wouldn't be where I am today;
- My dear parents, in-laws, grandparents and wider family in Israel and London for being an eternal source of love, hope and support;
- Peter Kann, my mentor and master's thesis advisor, for your wisdom and encouragement since we first met at Columbia Journalism School when you agreed to be my master's thesis advisor on an investigation into the under-explored role barbershops play in providing mental health support to men. I continue to be in awe of the tales from your career as a Pulitzer Prize-winning correspondent, former publisher of the *Wall Street Journal* and Chairman and CEO of *Dow Jones & Company*;
- Ari Goldman, for igniting my passion in journalism and giving the best 'Reporting 101' tutorial a novice could ask for;
- Tami Luhby, senior writer at CNN and my reporting professor at Columbia, for your inspiring support over the past seven years;
- Nigel Gee, for your immense support while I applied to study at Columbia Journalism School, where I discovered my love for the written word;

- Yaron Peleg, my director of studies at Jesus College, Cambridge University, for stirring my fascination with the Middle East in all its myriad complexities;
- Nathan Means, for your editorial wizardry as we turned these pages into a presentable manuscript;
- Howard Lovy, for your sage counsel in the early days of this book's creation; and Jay Mens and Gabriel Max, for your rigorous review and unvarnished feedback on multiple iterations of *Unveiled*.

ABOUT THE AUTHOR

Jonathan Harounoff is an acclaimed British-Iranian journalist now serving as Israel's international spokesperson to the United Nations. His writings and commentaries have appeared in several publications, including *The New York Post*, *The New York Times*, *The Los Angeles Times*, Fox News, Newsweek, BBC, *Haaretz*, *The Jerusalem Post*, *The Jewish Chronicle* and *The Forward*. He previously served as director of communications at a D.C. think tank focused on US security interests in the Middle East. Earlier, Jonathan held corporate communications roles for the chairman and CEO of a Fortune 500 company. He graduated from the Universities of Cambridge and Columbia with degrees in journalism, Arabic and Persian, and is also an alumnus of Harvard University where he studied international relations and diplomacy. He lives in New York City with his wife, Stephanie.

We hope you enjoyed reading this title from:

www.blackrosewriting.com

Subscribe to our mailing list – *The Rosevine* – and receive **FREE** books, daily deals, and stay current with news about upcoming releases and our hottest authors.
Scan the QR code below to sign up.

Already a subscriber? Please accept a sincere thank you for being a fan of Black Rose Writing authors.

View other Black Rose Writing titles at www.blackrosewriting.com/books and use promo code **PRINT** to receive a **20% discount** when purchasing.

www.ingramcontent.com/pod-product-compliance
Lightning Source LLC
Chambersburg PA
CBHW051828160426
43209CB00040B/1983/J